Marian Cox

# Jane Eyre

Anne Crow

LITERATURE

Philip Allan Updates, an imprint of Hodder Education, part of Hachette Livre UK, Market Place, Deddington, Oxfordshire OX15 0SE

*Orders*
Bookpoint Ltd, 130 Milton Park, Abingdon, Oxfordshire, OX14 4SB
tel: 01235 827720
fax: 01235 400454
e-mail: uk.orders@bookpoint.co.uk
Lines are open 9.00 a.m.–5.00 p.m., Monday to Saturday, with a 24-hour message answering service. You can also order through the Philip Allan Updates website: www.philipallan.co.uk

© Philip Allan Updates 2008

ISBN 978-0-340-96571-9

First printed 2008

Impression number   5   4   3   2   1

Year   2013   2012   2011   2010   2009   2008

In all cases we have attempted to trace and credit copyright owners of material used.

Printed in Malta

*Environmental information*
Hachette Livre UK's policy is to use papers that are natural, renewable and recyclable products and made from wood grown in sustainable forests. The logging and manufacturing processes are expected to conform to the environmental regulations of the country of origin.

# Contents

# Introduction

## Aims of the guide

The purpose of this Student Text Guide to Charlotte Brontë's classic novel *Jane Eyre* is to enable you to organise your thoughts and responses to the novel, to deepen your understanding of key features and aspects, and to help you to address the particular requirements of examination questions in order to obtain the best possible grade. It will also prove useful if you are writing a coursework piece on the novel as it provides a number of summaries, lists, analyses and references to help with the content and construction of your assignment.

It is assumed that you have read and studied the novel already under the guidance of a teacher or lecturer. This Student Text Guide is a revision guide, not an introduction, although some of its content serves the purpose of providing initial background. It can be read in its entirety in one sitting, or it can be dipped into and used as a reference guide to specific and separate aspects of the novel.

The *Text guidance* consists of a series of chapters that examine key aspects of the novel including contexts, interpretations and controversies.

The final section, *Questions and Answers*, gives examples of essay questions of different types and includes exemplar essay plans and samples of student work.

Note that the examiners are seeking above all else evidence of an *informed personal response* to the text. A revision guide such as this can help you to understand the text and to form your own opinions, and it can suggest areas to think about, but it cannot replace your own ideas and responses as an individual reader.

Page references in this guide refer to the 2006 Penguin Classics edition of the novel.

## Assessment Objectives

The revised Assessment Objectives for A-level English literature from 2008 are common to all boards:

| AO1 | Articulate creative, informed and relevant responses to literary texts, using appropriate terminology and concepts, and coherent, accurate written expression. |
|-----|------------------------------------------------------------------------------------------------------------------|
| AO2 | Demonstrate detailed critical understanding in analysing the ways in which structure, form and language shape meanings in literary texts. |

| AO3 | Explore connections and comparisons between different literary texts, informed by interpretations of other readers. |
|---|---|
| AO4 | Demonstrate understanding of the significance and influence of the contexts in which literary texts are written and received. |

# Writing examination essays

## Choosing the right question

The first skill you must show when presented with the exam paper is the ability to choose the more appropriate, for you, of the two questions on your text. It is unlikely, but possible, that a question contains a word with which you are unfamiliar, in which case it would be safer to choose the other one. Do not be tempted to choose a question because of its similarity to one you have already done. Freshness and thinking on the spot usually produce a better product than attempted recall of a previous essay that may have received only a mediocre mark in the first place. The exam question is unlikely to have exactly the same focus and your response may seem 'off centre' as a result, as well as stale and perfunctory in expression.

Essay questions fall into the following categories: close passage analysis and relation to whole text; characterisation; setting and atmosphere; structure and effectiveness; genre; language and style; themes and issues. Remember, however, that themes are relevant to all essays and that analysis, not just description, is always required. Exam titles are open ended in the sense that there is no obvious right answer, and you would therefore be unwise to give a dismissive, extreme or entirely one-sided response — the question would not have been set if the answer were not debatable. An ability and willingness to see both sides is an Assessment Objective and shows independence of judgement as a reader. Do not be afraid to explore the issues and do not try to tie the text into one neat interpretation. If there is ambiguity it is likely to be deliberate on the part of the author and must be discussed. Literary texts are complex and often paradoxical, and it would be a misreading of them to suggest that there is only one possible interpretation.

## Underlining key words

When you have chosen your question, underline the key words in the title. There may be only one or as many as five or six, and it is essential that you discover how many aspects your response has to cover and fix in your mind the focus the answer must have. An essay that answers only half the question cannot score top marks, however well that half is executed, and you need to demonstrate your responsiveness to all the implications of the question. The key words often provide the subheadings for planning and can suggest your overall approach to the essay.

## Planning and structuring

To be convincing, your essay must demonstrate a logical order of thought and a sense of progression towards a conclusion. If you reproduce your ideas in random order as they occur to you, they are unlikely to form a coherent whole. Jumping between unrelated ideas is confusing for the reader and weakens your argument.

The first stage of your essay plan, on which you can afford to spend seven to eight minutes, should be to brainstorm as a list all the appropriate ideas and material you can think of, in note form. You should aim for ten or 12 separate points which will become the ten or 12 paragraphs of your essay. If, after a few minutes, you do not have enough material, quickly switch to the other essay title. Beside each point, in a parallel column, indicate how you will support it. Next, group together the ideas that seem to belong together, and sort them into a logical order, using numbers. Identify which point will be the basis of your conclusion and move it to the end. The first points will follow from the essay title and definition of key words, and will be a springboard for your line of argument.

Remember that character, events and aspects of language exist as vehicles for a novel's themes — the real reason why texts are written. You need to become accustomed to planning by theme, using the other three elements to provide support and examples. Check with the Assessment Objectives printed on the exam paper that your plan covers all the necessary elements.

Passage questions need planning as much as general ones, and they are more in danger of slipping into plot narration rather than analysis and interpretation. Avoid running commentaries: texts should not automatically be treated chronologically but according to the argument you construct in answer to the question.

Your plan should be cancelled with one diagonal line when you have finished writing your essay. The examiner does not want to start reading it by mistake.

## Evidence

When selecting a point, check that you can support it adequately and convincingly. If not, substitute a better point. Unsupported assertion does not get much credit in exam essays and gives the impression of desperation or lack of familiarity with the text. Using about three paragraphs to a page, you should structure each paragraph by making a point and then supporting it with textual evidence, and a brief analysis of how it relates to the question.

Evidence for your argument can take three forms: reference, example or quotation. Aim for a mixture of these forms, as well as of different kinds of evidence (character, plot, image etc.); bear in mind that there is no need to support indisputable facts, for example that the narrator is Jane Rochester.

Do not be afraid of using too much quotation; up to a quarter of an essay, or one per sentence, is acceptable. However, quotation for the sake of it, without interpretation or relevance, is useless. You should aim for short, integrated quotations of two or three words rather than longer ones, which take time and space and are less effective. Short quotations (less than one line of printed text) can be incorporated into your own sentence; longer quotations need to be introduced by a colon and inset from both margins. If you are considering using such a lengthy quotation, pause and ask yourself if it is all necessary.

If you cannot think of the right quotation to prove a point, reconsider whether the point is valid or worth making, or you could use example or illustration instead. Sometimes there just is not an appropriate quotation. Remember that a quotation may prove more than one point. Rather than repeating it, which weakens its effect, use it as a 'sandwich' between the two ideas it illustrates, which gives the impression of clever structuring.

Remember that characters do not work in isolation and a full analysis of a passage usually requires at least passing references to several characters for purposes of comparison and contrast. Do not neglect the minor characters in the text — they may not appear to say or do much, but they must be there for a reason, perhaps to provide useful comments on the main characters, or to represent aspects of themes.

## Openings

Openings are the first indication to the examiner whether you are an excellent, middling or weak student. By the end of the first paragraph you will have revealed an ability to write relevantly, accurately, clearly — or not. For the most part, the best way in to a literature essay is to define the implications and complexities of the title, starting with the underlined keywords, especially if they are abstract concepts with a variety of possible interpretations (such as 'successful' and 'truth'). Next, the widest and broadest application of the terms to the text will produce a range of ideas that could themselves be the structural headings for the essay.

As well as indicating the scope and framework for the answer, the introduction should provide brief and relevant contextual information, including the setting of the scene if a passage question, or the general background for a whole-text answer. This may refer to the genre, the period, the themes or the main characters. Only points directly relevant to the question can be credited, so get started on the analysis as soon as possible.

## Writing

With a useful plan you can write continuously — without needing to stop and think what to say next — and with fluency and coherence. You will need to write quickly and legibly. Think about appropriate expression and accuracy, asking yourself always 'What exactly am I trying to say?' Try to sound engaged and enthusiastic in your response. Examiners are human and affected by tone as much as any reader is with any text. Learn and apply the mnemonic acronym ACRID (accurate, concise, relevant, interesting and detailed).

Each paragraph should follow logically from the one before, either to continue the argument or to change its direction. Adverbial paragraph links — such as 'Furthermore', 'However', 'On the other hand' — are vital pointers to the progression of the argument. Paragraphs are a necessary courtesy to the reader and an indicator of point/topic change. Paragraphs that are too long or too short reveal repetitive expression and lack of structure, or undeveloped ideas and lack of support respectively.

Avoid tentative or dogmatic statements, which make you sound either vague and uncertain or pompous and arrogant. Do not overstate or become sensational or emotional. Steer clear of cliché and 'waffle'. Use known literary conventions, such as discussing literature in the present tense, avoiding calling a reader 'he', and using the surnames of authors. In an exam essay, it is usually safer to discuss the text itself, rather than to speculate about the author's intentions or personal viewpoint.

Write in a suitably formal, objective and impersonal style, avoiding ambiguous, repetitive and vague phrases. The aim is always clarity of thought and expression. Use appropriate technical terms to show competence and save words, and choose exactly the right word and not the rough approximation that first comes to mind. Remember that every word should work for you and do not waste time on 'filler' expressions, such as 'As far as the novel is concerned', and adverbial intensifiers, such as 'totally' and 'indeed'. Say something once, explore it, prove it and move on. You can get credit for a point only once. It must always be clear how your point relates to the title, not left to the reader to guess or mind-read what you think the connection may be.

Do not speculate, hypothesise, exaggerate or ask questions — it is your job to answer them. Feelings are not a substitute for thought in an academic essay. Do not patronise the author by praising her for being clever or achieving something and do not parrot your teacher through your expression of an idea. The examiner will quickly spot if the whole class is using the same phrasing, and will then know it is not your own idea being expressed. To quote from examiners' comments, to achieve a grade A, candidates are required to 'show a freshness of personal response as opposed to mere repetition of someone else's critical opinions, however good'. Whether the examiner agrees with you or not is irrelevant; it is the quality of the argument that counts.

## Endings

The ending is what the whole essay has been working towards and what the examiner has in mind when deciding on a final mark. An ending needs to be conclusive, impressive and climactic, and not give the impression that you have run

out of time or ideas. An ineffective ending is often the result of poor planning. Just repeating a point already made or ending with a summary of the essay is a weak way of finishing, and cannot earn any extra marks.

Once again there are techniques for constructing conclusions. You need to take a step back from the close focus of the essay and make a comment that pulls together everything you have been saying and ties it into the overall significance of the text. A quotation from within or outside the text, possibly by the author, can be effective and definitive. You can also refer back to the title, or your opening statement, so that there is a satisfying sense of circularity for the reader, giving the impression that there is no more to be said on this subject.

## Checking

Writing fast always causes slips of the mind and pen, and unfortunately these missing letters and words, misnamings of characters and genre confusions, are indistinguishable from ignorance and therefore must be corrected. Also, you do not want to give away the fact that you did not bother to check your work, which will give a negative impression of your standards as a literature student. Examiners can always tell when work has been left unchecked.

When you check, you are no longer the writer but the reader of the text you have created, and a stranger too. Can you follow its line of argument? Are the facts accurate? Does it hang together? Is the vocabulary explicit? Is everything supported? Most importantly, does it actually answer the question? Obviously you also need to watch out for spelling, grammar and punctuation errors, as well as continuing until the last second to improve the content and the expression.

## Summary

There is no such thing as a perfect or model essay; flawed essays can gain full marks. There is always something more that could have been said, and examiners realise that students have limitations when writing under pressure in timed conditions. You are not penalised for what you did not say in comparison to a conceptual ideal answer, but rewarded for the knowledge and understanding you have managed to demonstrate. It is not as difficult as you may think to do well, provided that you are very familiar with the text and have sufficient essay-writing experience. Follow the process of choose, underline, select, support, structure, write and check, and you cannot go far wrong.

Text Guidance

LITERATURE

# Contexts
## Biographical details

There is no doubt that Charlotte Brontë drew upon her own experiences for her novel *Jane Eyre*, and that its power comes from the fact that she poured her own passionate feelings into her heroine. However, it is not autobiographical. Petite, plain, well read and clever, Charlotte, like Jane, was a strong woman with an overwhelming capacity for love, a deep religious faith, and a well-developed sense of duty. Unlike Jane, however, she grew up in a very close-knit family.

She was the third of six children born to the Reverend Patrick Brontë and his wife, Maria. Patrick Brontë, son of an illiterate Irish tenant farmer, was a brilliant and determined man who managed, against all the odds, to get a scholarship to Cambridge University, where he was sponsored by William Wilberforce, the anti-slavery campaigner. He changed his name from Punty to Brontë, meaning 'thunder' in Greek — a significant choice, and one that can be seen as part of his desire to hide his humble origins. He was ordained in 1806, and in 1820 he was given the perpetual curacy of Haworth, on the Yorkshire moors. This was expected to be a step up in a glittering career, and the fact that he stayed is testament to his commitment to his parishioners and his determination to improve their lives. Charlotte Brontë was five years old when the family moved to Haworth, but soon afterwards her mother died of cancer.

The children were then cared for by their aunt, Elizabeth Branwell, who had come from Cornwall to nurse her sister. Many cruel myths about Patrick Brontë were started by the disgruntled nurse who lost her position with the arrival of Elizabeth. These were picked up by Charlotte Brontë's friend, Elizabeth Gaskell, who included them in her biography, and so they are often found in modern studies of the Brontës. Those who knew him well — friends, servants and parishioners — all agree that he was a devoted husband and father, a kind and affable man. Presumably, Mrs Gaskell wished to offer his eccentricity as an excuse for those unconventional aspects of Charlotte Brontë's writing that many Victorians found unacceptable, such as Jane's unusually frank accounts of her feelings for Mr Rochester.

All the evidence supports the fact that the children had a happy, normal, stable childhood, with an affectionate aunt and a father willing to spend time with them and join in their games. The children always read avidly and their father allowed them free run of his library, which, of course, included his own published works, and all the newspapers and periodicals that came into the house. He did not censor their reading material at all, so they read works that, at the time, were considered too immoral for ladies, such as Byron's *Don Juan*. Patrick Brontë was not only a respected writer, he was also a tireless campaigner for social reform, so his children were certainly not isolated from the world and its problems, nor from the appalling poverty that surrounded them.

## School

When Aunt Branwell expressed a wish to return to Cornwall, it was decided to send the older girls to school. Patrick Brontë's salary was small, so, after careful consideration, he chose a new school, Cowan Bridge, specifically designed for the daughters of clergymen and supported by many eminent people, including Patrick's former university friend and sponsor William Wilberforce. Although Charlotte's account of Jane's time at Lowood Institution is clearly based on her own experiences, it is enhanced by scandalous reports of other schools she had read in newspapers, and the picture is a caricature, written through the eyes of a child who clearly resented the school.

Nevertheless, it is true that the girls were unfortunate to be at the school during its difficult early years and, as at Lowood, there was an outbreak of typhus that seems to have masked the fact that Charlotte Brontë's older sisters, Maria and Elizabeth, were suffering from tuberculosis. Charlotte Brontë has said that the character of Helen Burns, whom many critics have found too good to be true, was based on Maria, whom she described as having a 'prematurely developed and remarkable intellect, as well as…mildness, wisdom and fortitude'. As soon as Patrick knew of their illnesses, he took all four girls home, but Maria and Elizabeth did not recover. This was clearly a sadness that affected Charlotte deeply, and it also gave her a new sense of duty and responsibility, now that she was the oldest in the family.

After this tragedy, Aunt Branwell stayed and the children were educated at home. As well as their lessons, they practised drawing by copying pictures such as the engravings in Bewick's *History of British Birds*. They supplemented their father's library with books from libraries and borrowed periodicals. One in particular, *Blackwood's Magazine*, a miscellany of satire and comment on contemporary politics and literature, was a strong formative influence, providing characters and settings for many of their games. Like most children, they played with their toys imaginatively, giving the dolls and soldiers characters and inventing stories for them. They made up plays, acting them out exuberantly and writing down their adventures. These plays developed into a complex imaginary world with two kingdoms: Charlotte and Branwell created Angria, and Emily and Anne, Gondal. They made tiny books out of scraps of paper, and they imitated print in writing so small that it was like a code that adults would not be able to read without a magnifying glass.

Mrs Gaskell was wrong to assume that the Brontë children's interests were 'of a sedentary and intellectual nature'. They vigorously acted out their characters' battles in the garden and played freely on the moors. They were not isolated, but

happy in each other's company, so that they did not need playmates. They were also very aware of what was happening in the world at large, and they incorporated real people and events into their stories. These imaginary worlds were by no means a simple retreat from reality, but a source of endless fun, which they still enjoyed when they were adults. The books, as one would expect, were strongly derivative as they imitated those writers they enjoyed, such as Lord Byron and Sir Walter Scott. Charlotte Brontë used her characters to poke fun at her brother and sisters, developing the satirical skills she was to use in *Jane Eyre*.

The greatest gifts Patrick Brontë gave his children were a thirst for education and the freedom, as far as he could afford, to find it wherever they could. Although their formal education was partial and fragmented, the Brontës came from a household where all kinds of artistic pursuit were encouraged. They tried their hands at everything, shared everything and explored human feelings in a way that would not have been possible without siblings who were kindred spirits.

## Responsibility

In 1830, Patrick Brontë fell seriously ill, and this brought home to the family the fact that, if he were to die, the children would have no home and no income. At 14, Charlotte Brontë was again sent away to school to equip her to earn her own living. She was sent to Roe Head, where she soon settled in and made lifelong friends. She took her responsibility to improve herself seriously and was soon top of her class. Being extremely short-sighted, she could not play ball games nor read the music while she played an instrument, but she soon found her forte, telling horror stories in the dormitory after lights out and organising plays. Her two best friends, Ellen Nussey and Mary Taylor, often invited her to their homes for long weekends or short holidays, and they remained close for the rest of her life.

Ellen and Mary appealed to the contrasting aspects of Charlotte Brontë's personality that are central to *Jane Eyre*. Ellen accepted the current social and moral codes, reconciling herself to a life of duty and dependence; Charlotte strove to emulate her in her peaceful acceptance of her fate as a poor clergyman's daughter, unlikely ever to marry. In contrast, Mary Taylor was intellectually curious and totally careless of the opinions of others. Mary's letters and her example stimulated Charlotte to use her abilities and talents to the full and to question the prejudices of society. Faced with the prospect of life as poor spinsters, Ellen lived quietly on her brother's charity but Mary emigrated to New Zealand so that she could engage in business and made enough money to return and live in comfortable independence.

At 16, Charlotte Brontë left Roe Head and returned to Haworth to take responsibility for educating her younger sisters, slipping back easily into their imaginary kingdoms of Gondal and Angria. In 1835, however, she accepted a position as teacher at Roe Head, where she stayed until 1838. Disliking teaching, she made her first attempt to embark on a literary career; she sent some of her poems to the Poet Laureate, Robert Southey. His reply reflected the prejudices of the time: 'Literature cannot be the business of a woman's life and it ought not to be. The more she is engaged in her proper duties, the less leisure will she have for it, even as an accomplishment and a recreation.' No wonder Jane speaks so feelingly in Chapter XII: 'Women feel just as men feel; they need exercise for their faculties, and a field for their efforts as much as their brothers do.' At the time, however, Charlotte Brontë took Southey's advice to heart, shelved her literary ambitions temporarily, and went back to teaching.

Nevertheless, she continued to write the imaginary stories of Angria. In her love stories the women fall abjectly in love with her imaginary hero, the Duke of Zamorna, who treats them with an amused and cynical contempt. Mr Rochester certainly owes something to his fictional predecessor but, unlike her Gondal stories, Charlotte rebukes him through Jane for his treatment of his mistresses and Blanche, and demands his pity for Bertha. *Jane Eyre* blends this romantic world of Charlotte's imagination with her sense of duty and her strong religious faith. When she was made a proposal of marriage by Ellen's brother, she rejected her suitor because, not only would she have lost her precious independence, but also, like Jane, she needed to love her husband and to be loved by him.

Instead, she took a series of positions as governess, where she gained more material for her novel. Charlotte Brontë hated the fact that she was treated as a servant, not just teaching the children but having to amuse them and do menial tasks. She found it exhausting and depressing to be constantly in demand, and she was doubtless a reluctant and melancholy governess. Still believing that she could not make her living by writing, the only escape seemed to be for the sisters to set up their own school at Haworth.

## Pensionnat Heger

Accordingly, in 1842, Charlotte and Emily Brontë went to a school in Brussels for 18 months to improve their language skills for teaching, and Charlotte returned later as a teacher. It was here that she learnt the rigours of the academic discipline needed for writing, and here that she experienced the passion that she had dreamt of for her heroines, falling in love with a man who, however, was the opposite of her imaginary heroes. Charlotte wrote in a letter that the husband of Madame Heger, the director of the school, was 'a man of power as to mind, but very choleric and irritable as to temperament; a little black ugly being'. She knew that he held her in high regard as one of his star pupils. It was the first time someone outside the family, whose judgement she respected and whose intellect was equal, if not superior, to her own, had recognised and encouraged her talent. Gradually she became obsessively dependent on his approval, and, even after she was sent away by Madame Heger, she continued to write to him, declaring her passion and describing her anguish at being 'slave to a regret, a memory, slave to a dominating

and fixed idea which tyrannises one's spirit'. The lyrics of the song Mr Rochester sings in Chapter XXIV were written for Monsieur Heger.

In 1845, Charlotte's hopes of being a published writer were rekindled when she found a book of poems by her sister, Emily. The three sisters submitted a combined anthology, under the pseudonyms of Currer, Ellis and Acton Bell, partly to preserve anonymity, but also because they 'had a vague impression that authoresses are liable to be looked on with prejudice'. When these failed to sell, each sister started to write a novel. Charlotte Brontë's first novel, *The Professor*, based heavily on her Angria stories and her experiences in Brussels, was rejected by a succession of publishers, but one of them encouraged her to continue writing. For her next novel, *Jane Eyre*, Charlotte Brontë drew on personal experience for her characters and her settings, and she chose a woman as her narrator.

## Literary success

In *Jane Eyre*, Charlotte Brontë used local stories of mad wives locked away, and she based the descriptions of the buildings where Jane lived on houses she had visited. She drew on her experiences at school and as a governess. She based St John's proposal of marriage on the one she had received from Reverend Henry Nussey, who explained that he had chosen Charlotte because he intended to take pupils and needed a wife to take care of them. More important, however, she could finally release all the pent-up feelings of her love for Monsieur Heger, her anger and grief at Cowan Bridge School for her sisters' deaths, and her bitter resentment and sense of injustice at the way she had been treated as a governess. These strong emotions gave the novel a new and compelling power, which made it an instant success. She wrote a preface to the second edition, answering critics who declared it was an 'improper' book and dedicating the novel to her literary hero, William Makepeace Thackeray.

Almost a year after *Jane Eyre* was published, Charlotte Brontë's brother, Branwell, died of tuberculosis, complicated by alcoholism. A few weeks later, Emily died, followed a few months later by Anne — both of them also dying of tuberculosis. Caring alone for her elderly father, Charlotte Brontë continued to write, publishing *Shirley* in 1849 and *Villette* in 1853. Eventually she found the love she craved, and she married Arthur Bell Nicholls, her father's curate, in 1854. She rejected him at first, as she had three earlier suitors, but he finally won her round, in spite of her father's objections. Sadly, their happiness did not last long, as Charlotte and the child she was carrying died in 1855.

# Chronology

| Date | Historical events | Charlotte's life | Literature |
|------|-------------------|------------------|------------|
| 1776 | American Declaration of Independence | | |
| 1784 | James Watt invents the steam engine | | |
| 1785 | Edmund Cartwright invents the power loom | | |
| 1787 | Association for the Abolition of the Slave Trade founded | | |
| 1789 | French Revolution; Declaration of the Rights of Man | | |
| 1792 | | | Mary Wollstonecraft: *A Vindication of the Rights of Women* |
| 1793 | Execution of Louis XVI; Reign of Terror; Britain and France at war | | Godwin: *Political Justice* |
| 1794 | Habeas Corpus suspended in Britain | | Mrs Radcliffe: *The Mysteries of Udolpho* |
| 1798 | Nelson's victory at the Battle of the Nile; rebellion in Ireland | | Wordsworth and Coleridge: *Lyrical Ballads*; Wollstonecraft: *The Wrongs of Women* |
| 1801 | Habeas Corpus again suspended; Inclosure Consolidation Act passed | | |
| 1805 | Nelson's victory at Trafalgar | | Walter Scott: *The Lay of the Last Minstrel* |
| 1807 | Abolition of slave trade in British Empire | | Wordsworth: *Poems* |
| 1808 | Peninsular War begins | | Scott: *Marmion* |
| 1810 | | | Patrick Brontë: *Cottage Poems* |

| Date | Historical events | Charlotte's life | Literature |
| --- | --- | --- | --- |
| 1811 | Prince of Wales becomes Regent; Luddite riots | | Jane Austen: *Sense and Sensibility* |
| 1812 | French retreat from Moscow | Revd Patrick Brontë marries Maria Branwell | Lord Byron: *Childe Harold's Pilgrimage* |
| 1813 | | | Austen: *Pride and Prejudice*; Patrick Brontë: *The Rural Minstrel: A Miscellany of Descriptive Poems* |
| 1814 | Abdication of Napoleon; Restoration of Louis XVIII; Stephenson's steam locomotive | Maria born | Wordsworth: *Excursion*; Byron: *The Corsair*; Austen: *Mansfield Park*; Scott: *Waverley* |
| 1815 | Battle of Waterloo; Importation Act passed to protect corn prices from cheap imports, keeping price of bread high | Elizabeth born | Wordsworth: *Poems*; Byron: *Completed Works*; Patrick Brontë: *The Cottage in the Wood* |
| 1816 | Game Laws passed | Charlotte born: 21 April | Coleridge: *Christabel* and *Kubla Khan*; Shelley: *Alastor*; Austen: *Emma* |
| 1817 | Habeas Corpus suspended; Jane Austen dies | Branwell born | Byron: *Manfred*; Keats: *Poems* |
| 1818 | Habeas Corpus restored | Emily born | Patrick Brontë: *The Maid of Killarney*; Austen: *Northanger Abbey* and *Persuasion*; Scott: *The Heart of Midlothian*; Mary Shelley: *Frankenstein*; Keats: *Endymion* |
| 1819 | Peterloo Massacre | | Byron: *Don Juan*; Scott: *The Bride of Lammermoor* |
| 1820 | Death of George III; accession of George IV | January: Anne born April: family settles at Haworth | Shelley: *Prometheus Unbound*; Keats: *Eve of St Agnes*; Scott: *Ivanhoe* |
| 1821 | Greek War of Independence; Keats dies | Mrs Brontë ill; her sister nurses her April: Mrs Brontë dies | Byron: *Cain*; Shelley: *Adonais* |

| Date | Historical events | Charlotte's life | Literature |
|------|-------------------|------------------|------------|
| 1822 | Shelley dies | | Byron: *The Vision of Judgement* |
| 1824 | Byron dies | July: Maria, Elizabeth, Charlotte and Emily go to Cowan Bridge School | Scott: *Redgauntlet* |
| 1825 | Financial crisis: opening of Stockton and Darlington Railway | Maria and Elizabeth die; Charlotte and Emily brought home in June | |
| 1829 | Catholic Emancipation Act | | |
| 1830 | Death of George IV; accession of William IV; opening of Manchester and Liverpool Railway | | Tennyson: *Poems, Chiefly Lyrical* |
| 1831 | Cholera epidemic; unsuccessful introduction of Reform Bills; riots | January: Charlotte to school at Roe Head | |
| 1832 | Reform Act; Walter Scott dies; a Sunday school started at Haworth | July: Charlotte returns to Haworth to teach her sisters | Tennyson: *Poems*; Harriet Martineau: *Illustrations of Political Economy* |
| 1834 | Abolition of slavery | | |
| 1835 | Municipal Reform Act | July: Charlotte goes to teach at Roe Head | Browning: *Paracelsus* |
| 1836 | | Charlotte sends her poems to Southey | Dickens: *Sketches by Boz*; *Pickwick Papers* |
| 1837 | Death of William IV; accession of Victoria | Southey sends a patronising reply | Carlyle: *French Revolution*; Dickens: *Oliver Twist* |
| 1838 | *People's Charter* published; London to Birmingham Railway opened | Charlotte leaves Roe Head School | Dickens: *Nicholas Nickleby* |
| 1839 | Chartist's petition rejected by Parliament | Charlotte rejects two proposals of marriage; first experience as governess | Carlyle: *Chartism* |

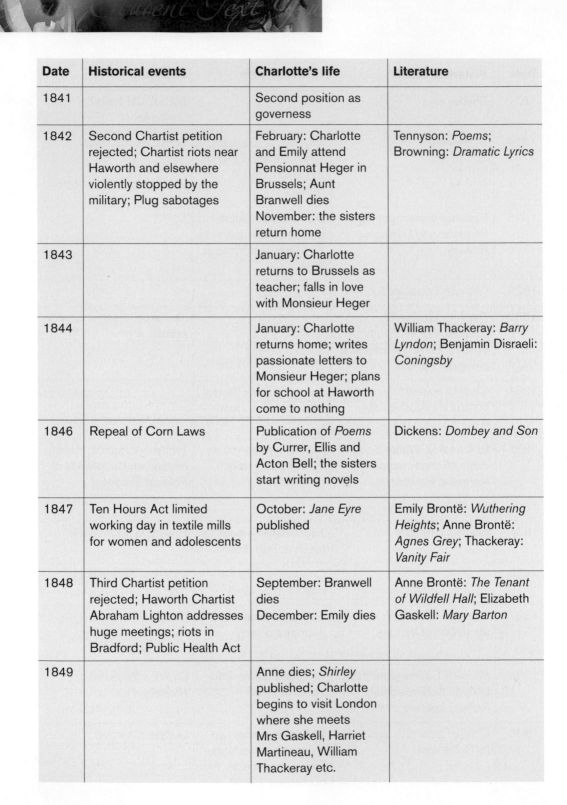

| Date | Historical events | Charlotte's life | Literature |
|------|-------------------|------------------|------------|
| 1841 | | Second position as governess | |
| 1842 | Second Chartist petition rejected; Chartist riots near Haworth and elsewhere violently stopped by the military; Plug sabotages | February: Charlotte and Emily attend Pensionnat Heger in Brussels; Aunt Branwell dies November: the sisters return home | Tennyson: *Poems*; Browning: *Dramatic Lyrics* |
| 1843 | | January: Charlotte returns to Brussels as teacher; falls in love with Monsieur Heger | |
| 1844 | | January: Charlotte returns home; writes passionate letters to Monsieur Heger; plans for school at Haworth come to nothing | William Thackeray: *Barry Lyndon*; Benjamin Disraeli: *Coningsby* |
| 1846 | Repeal of Corn Laws | Publication of *Poems* by Currer, Ellis and Acton Bell; the sisters start writing novels | Dickens: *Dombey and Son* |
| 1847 | Ten Hours Act limited working day in textile mills for women and adolescents | October: *Jane Eyre* published | Emily Brontë: *Wuthering Heights*; Anne Brontë: *Agnes Grey*; Thackeray: *Vanity Fair* |
| 1848 | Third Chartist petition rejected; Haworth Chartist Abraham Lighton addresses huge meetings; riots in Bradford; Public Health Act | September: Branwell dies December: Emily dies | Anne Brontë: *The Tenant of Wildfell Hall*; Elizabeth Gaskell: *Mary Barton* |
| 1849 | | Anne dies; *Shirley* published; Charlotte begins to visit London where she meets Mrs Gaskell, Harriet Martineau, William Thackeray etc. | |

| Date | Historical events | Charlotte's life | Literature |
|------|-------------------|------------------|------------|
| 1850 | Babbage: *Report to the General Board of Health* | | E. B. Browning: *Sonnets from the Portuguese* |
| 1851 | The Great Exhibition at Crystal Palace | | |
| 1852 | Duke of Wellington dies | Patrick Brontë's curate, Arthur Bell Nicholls, proposes marriage; father opposed; Charlotte refuses Nicholls | Harriet Beecher Stowe: *Uncle Tom's Cabin* |
| 1853 | | *Villette* published | |
| 1854 | Crimean War breaks out (ends 1856); Working Man's College opened | Charlotte marries Nicholls, becomes pregnant | |
| 1855 | | 31 March, Charlotte dies | |
| 1857 | Indian Mutiny | *The Professor* (Charlotte's first novel) published | Gaskell: *The Life of Charlotte Brontë* |
| 1861 | | Patrick Brontë dies | |

# Historical, political and social overview

The nineteenth century was a time of great change:

- There were intense debates about religious issues, not least the question of who should hold authority in matters of religion.
- It was also a time of social reorganisation and the transfer of power as a new wealthy middle class, created by the Industrial Revolution, emerged to challenge the dominance of the traditional landowners.
- It was a time of heated controversy over ideas of democracy and political rights, fuelled by such significant events in the world as American Independence with its Declaration of Human Rights, and the French Revolution with its ideas of liberty, equality and fraternity.
- There was growing unrest among the working classes, who demanded relief from the appalling conditions in which they had to live and work, and this gradually became a matter of concern among higher classes.

The government, fearing that revolution would break out in Britain as well as abroad, responded with repressive legislation rather than trying to improve matters. Several times the government suspended Habeas Corpus, which is the right not to be imprisoned without trial. There was a determination to protect and defend the landed interest, which was the basis of the government's political power. Common land on which people used to have the right to graze their animals was enclosed. Corn Laws were introduced to keep the price of grain high for landowners and to prevent the import of cheap grain from abroad, which kept the price of bread high. Game Laws were passed, meaning that anyone catching a rabbit, for example, to feed a starving family, could be transported for seven years. The government brought in the military to suppress civil rights demonstrations; the most widely known example of this is popularly called the Peterloo Massacre, in which 18 people were killed and 500 wounded when the yeomanry used sabres to break up a meeting on St Peter's Fields near Manchester.

Nevertheless, pressure for reform grew and the first Reform Act was passed in 1832. This effected some minor improvements, but ordinary working men were still without a vote. The demand for universal male suffrage and a secret ballot acted as a rallying standard for working-class agitation throughout the country. Marches, rallies, speeches and petitions were organised in support of it. Eventually, in 1884, the Third Reform Act was passed, giving the vote to male householders and lodgers who had been resident for 12 months. This still left a third of all men (including soldiers in barracks, policemen and domestic servants) without the vote. It was not until 1918 that Britain achieved universal male suffrage, and women were not given the vote until 1928.

The nineteenth century was not a time of change for women, although there was much debate on the Woman Question. The role of women in society had been questioned in the eighteenth century by, among others, Mary Wollstonecraft, who argued that women were not naturally submissive but taught to be so, confined to 'snarling under the lash at which [they] dare not snarl' (*A Vindication of the Rights of Women*). Whereas, thanks to the industrialisation and the growth of the servant class, more working-class women than ever before worked outside the home, middle-class women in the nineteenth century were allowed no economically productive careers. They were not permitted to go to university, to enter the learned professions or to engage in business. They were permitted to teach, but teachers and governesses were poorly paid and looked down upon by society.

# Industrial Revolution

In the early eighteenth century, the British textile industry was based largely on wool, which was spun and woven by outworkers in their own homes. Spinning wheels and handlooms can produce only a limited amount, and the quality is not always consistent, so technology was invented to improve efficiency. As large, powered machines were developed that led to a dramatic increase in production, it became more efficient to house them in mills, and so, towards the end of the eighteenth century, the textile industry was revolutionised. The increased demand for wool led landowners to evict their tenants so they could rear sheep. The outworkers found themselves unemployed, and many weavers, calling themselves Luddites after Ned Ludd, the Leicestershire man who had led the first rioters in the destruction of machinery, took out their resentment on the machines. Many people moved to the towns in search of work.

There was famine in Ireland, and desperately hungry people flocked into England, looking for work and prepared to take very low wages. Thomas Carlyle wrote in his essay, *Chartism*, that because of them wages were brought down to the equivalent of 'thirty weeks of third-rate potatoes', which was a man's yearly salary in Ireland. This meant that whole families had to work to earn enough to keep them alive. The poor mill workers had no hope of changing the system through the political process, since only landowners had the right to vote, so a movement arose to bring about change by other, more direct, means. These people drew up a six-point charter and became known as the Chartists. Gradually the industry became regulated. In 1833 and 1844, for instance, the first laws concerning child labour were passed. The 'improvements' were that no child under the age of nine was permitted to work in factories, children were no longer allowed to work at night, nor were they allowed to work longer than 12 hours a day.

## Haworth

The Brontë's home, Haworth, was a comparatively small town in the middle of the West Riding woollen industry, but it was an important one because it lay on one of the main routes between Yorkshire and Lancashire. Raw wool was transported through Haworth to Bradford to be treated and then taken to Halifax or Huddersfield to be made into cloth. Haworth is situated in the hills above Keighley and Bradford, with an ample supply of water, so it was an ideal place to site factories. When the Brontës moved to Haworth in 1820, it already had 13 small textile mills, as well as a large number of hand-loom weavers working in their own homes and a substantial cottage industry of wool combing. With the aftermath of the Napoleonic Wars and the industrial movement from the rural districts to the town, the population was rising sharply, bringing unemployment, misery and revolt.

Living conditions were primitive. The workers and their families lived in small houses in cramped streets. We know from the Babbage Report that, even in 1850, there was no sanitation at all, no sewers and few covered drains. The liquid waste, including that from privies, ran along open channels and gutters down the streets, and solid waste, including the refuse from privies, was thrown into walled enclosures in the backyards, known as middensteads. These were emptied by farmers and used to manure their fields, but sometimes the middensteads would overflow, creating an even worse health hazard. There were no water closets in Haworth and only 69 privies, one of which was at the rectory. With most households sharing a privy with up to 23 other families, it is not surprising that the mortality rates were among the highest in the country.

There was no running water in Haworth, so people had to fetch it from one of the few pumps, and in summer the pumps ran so slowly that people had to start queuing in the middle of the night to get water for the morning. The rectory was lucky enough to have its own pump in the kitchen, and, in his diary for September 1847, Patrick Brontë notes: 'Had the well cleaned out. It had not been cleaned for 20 years. The water was tinged yellow by eight tin cans in a state of decomposition.' If this was the state of a private well, it is horrifying to imagine the state of public ones. As a result of these insanitary conditions, four out of ten children died before reaching their sixth birthday, and the average age at death was 25. Whenever the wool trade was struggling, conditions grew even worse for the poor. In May 1830, for example, when Charlotte Brontë was 14, about two-thirds of the workers of Haworth were unemployed and the rest on short weeks. Patrick Brontë's strenuous efforts to raise public subscription for the relief of the poor always failed because it was felt that relief should be given from public rates and not private charity.

On 14 August 1842, about 10,000 people gathered at a Chartists' rally on Lees Moor, within sight and sound of Haworth. The military was called out to disperse the meeting, arresting and even shooting some of the demonstrators. A couple of weeks later, desperate mill workers sabotaged machinery by removing the plugs that powered the looms, which led to the formation of the Anti-Plug Dragoon Regiment. In Chapter XXXI of *Jane Eyre*, Brontë mentions the demonstrations when Rosamond Oliver tells St John that she has been dancing with the officers of the —th regiment, brought in to suppress the riots.

## Charlotte Brontë

Charlotte Brontë was surrounded by misery, and she could not have stepped out of her front door without seeing the suffering of the poor. Windows in the rectory looked out onto the graveyard, where she would see the frequent burials. She may even have heard the Haworth Chartist, Abraham Lighton, address the crowds, or seen the military brought in to keep the riots under control. After demonstrations in 1848, she wrote in a letter that the government should 'examine carefully into their causes of complaint and make such concessions as justice and humanity dictate'. Nevertheless, she was not a revolutionary. In the same year she wrote to her former headmistress: 'convulsive revolutions put back the world in all that is good, check civilisation, bring the dregs of society to the surface…That England may be spared the spasms, cramps, and frenzy-fits now contorting the Continent and threatening Ireland, I earnestly pray!'

## Class consciousness

However, the social effects of the Industrial Revolution were not all negative. For the energetic and enterprising few it offered opportunities for wealth that lifted former working-class men up to a new middle class. From here they could socialise with and marry into the old-established landed gentry and aristocracy. Brontë illustrates this through Mr Oliver, whose father had been a journeyman needlemaker but who was now able to boast that his daughter, Rosamond, had married the grandson and heir to the aristocrat, Sir Frederick Granby. The tension created by these two sets of values is central to *Jane Eyre*. On the one hand, there are rationality, rebellion and individualism; on the other hand, are tradition, conservatism and piety. Class consciousness pervades every part of the story. Jane's mother was from landed gentry, but she married beneath her, a poor clergyman, so Jane struggles against her poverty to maintain the status she believes is her right. Mr Rochester, 'an avowed republican', is a member of the landed gentry, and he now scorns a marriage for social reasons.

Charlotte's own position was even more precarious than that of her heroine, as her father came from Irish peasantry. Perhaps this is why she portrays Jane as reluctant to fall back, in social terms. Jane seems snobbish when she confides in her readers that, in her new position as schoolmistress she felt degraded. It is interesting that, ten years after the event, when she supposedly writes her autobiography, Jane is still writing in the present tense: 'Let me not despise myself too much for these feelings. I know them to be wrong — that is a great step gained; I shall strive to overcome them.' The use of the future tense may suggest that the conflict in Jane's mind is one that Charlotte herself had not fully resolved. It seems that, rationally, Charlotte believed in equality, but all her life she had been striving to lift herself out of the social position into which she was born, and she had not managed to reconcile the conflict between the deeply embedded traditional social mores and the radical views she had acquired.

## Governesses

As wealth shifted from the traditional landowners to the owners of industrial and mercantile enterprise, the latter not only began to challenge the privileges and superior social status of the upper class but also to consolidate their position against the threat from the working classes. They used institutions such as the Church and the school to keep those whom they regarded as social inferiors in their place. In *Jane Eyre*, Mr Brocklehurst and Mrs Reed work together to keep the poor orphan downtrodden, and to try to instil humility, obedience and respect. The new industrial middle classes also exploited the offspring of the impoverished gentry by employing them as tutors or governesses in order to lift their own children up above the class into which their parents had been born. A governess was in a lonely position because she was superior in class and education to the other servants, and she felt culturally superior to her employer. However, she was treated as a servant, required not only to teach the children and to keep them occupied but also to perform other jobs that her employer might give her. It is Mr Rochester who voices Brontë's opinion of 'this governessing slavery' (Chapter XXIV). On the one hand, Charlotte was a realist, recognising the need to earn her own living and wanting independence by whatever means she could gain it. On the other hand, she had a creative imagination, which gave her a feeling of superiority over those with less intellect than herself. Charlotte reveals how difficult she herself found it to reconcile the two, as her heroine finds herself torn between reason and feeling, realism and imagination.

# The position of women in Victorian society

When the novel was published in 1847, there was a queen on the throne of England, but this made no difference to the legal and economic position of other women. They had little more power or standing than children. No woman could vote and the law ignored them. Legally, a woman belonged to her nearest male relative. When a woman married, any property she had became her husband's and, if she earned any money, that was her husband's also. She would have been expected to address her husband by his full title rather than his Christian name, at least in front of other people. If she did not marry, after her father's death she became a dependant of her nearest male relative, and, as Bessie tells Jane, to be a dependant was to be 'less than a servant for you do nothing for your keep' (Chapter II). Working-class women could work in poor conditions on farms or in factories, but wages were too low for them to achieve any independence. A middle-class woman was expected to stay at home until she married and then spend the rest of her life looking after her family. If, like Charlotte Brontë and her heroine, a woman did not come from a wealthy family, and circumstances meant that she had to earn her own living, she could either be a governess in a family or a teacher in a school.

## Education

There was usually no opportunity for working-class girls to gain any formal education at all, but Charlotte Brontë shows in Rosamond Oliver's school that this situation was beginning to change. Middle-class girls were usually educated by governesses, while their brothers went to boarding school or had a more highly educated tutor. Girls were taught various social accomplishments to impress prospective suitors and to occupy their time, but their minds were not stretched and they were not expected to take these pursuits seriously. Bessie tells Jane 'of beautiful paintings of landscapes and flowers by [the young ladies] executed; of songs they could sing and pieces they could play, of purses they could net, of French books they could translate' (Chapter III). When the poet laureate, Robert Southey, discouraged Brontë from attempting a literary career, as it would take her away from her womanly duties, he was voicing the prejudice of the time. Charlotte Brontë's rejection of this view can be seen not only in her own published works, but also in the fact that Jane paints to express her imagination and individuality rather than to create a portfolio to impress an employer. However, when Jane chooses a school for Adèle, she conforms by selecting one which made her 'a pleasing and obliging companion: docile, good-tempered, and well-principled' (Chapter XXXVIII).

There were a few boarding schools, usually to educate poor children to become governesses, but the education they offered was far below the standard expected at boys' schools. In 1847, Queen's College for women was opened, offering the possibility of higher education for a few, but this was connected with the Governess Institution and aimed to train young women to teach. Nevertheless, it did make young women aware of their potential, and it provoked them to question and challenge the restrictions placed on their lives in a male-dominated society.

At the time Brontë started to write, some middle-class women were writing novels of what were deemed to be appropriately feminine genres: Gothic romances, society novels and moral tales. The Victorians, however, considered women's intellects to be weak, and their experience of life narrow, so women's writing was not valued highly. Charlotte Brontë blended these genres with the Romantic, satirical and social reformist novels that the men were writing to produce *Jane Eyre*, a novel which was unique, challenging and controversial.

## Expectations of women's behaviour *Jane Eyre*

In Chapter XII there is a strongly worded demand for equality with men that reveals the social expectations of women's behaviour in the middle of the nineteenth century. A woman was supposed to be passive, quiet and obedient, entirely subject to the authority of her male protector. A woman's intellect was presumed to be inferior to a man's, and she was not supposed to be ambitious or to aspire to anything more than being a wife and mother. English women were not expected to show any strong emotion such as anger or love, and it was most definitely assumed that they did not feel any sexual desire. Foreign women, however, were considered to be more highly sexed, and it is significant that Rochester's mistresses were all foreign.

In the Victorian age, women were idealised as the custodians of family values. While men could go out and 'enjoy' themselves, women stayed at home, upholding morality and truth, remaining uncontaminated by male desire, providing a calm and virtuous refuge for the man to return to. In *Jane Eyre*, Charlotte Brontë challenges these contemporary assumptions by offering a heroine who is at least as intelligent and passionate as Mr Rochester, and who seems to surpass him in intellectual and artistic aspirations.

# Religion

The early chapters of *Jane Eyre* give a clear impression of the way religion was taught in the nineteenth century. After Jane's passionate outburst, Miss Abbott tells Bessie: 'God will punish her: He might strike her dead in the midst of her tantrums', and to Jane she says: 'if you don't repent, something bad might be permitted to come down the chimney and fetch you away.' Jane has been well indoctrinated; she tells Mr Brocklehurst that hell is 'a pit full of fire' into which the wicked fall and where they burn for ever (Chapter II).

The nineteenth-century Church taught that 'Every soul that has ever lived must appear before the High Court of Heaven to be judged' (Ecclesiastes 12:14, Romans 14:12, Hebrews 9:27). 'Every motive, thought, word and deed will be under close scrutiny in the Day of Judgement' (Matthew 12:36, Revelation 20:12). Although God was deemed to be merciful, in the interest of universal justice He was still expected to punish every unrepentant sinner on the Day of Judgement. For the obedient believer, it was promised that this day would usher in eternal glory, but the unbeliever was warned that it would be a day of anguish and annihilation.

For people living in the first half of the nineteenth century, death was an integral part of life. They never knew where it would strike, nor how quickly, so it was important to them to prepare for the afterlife. The Church exploited this fear in an attempt to make people submissive and uncomplaining. For the majority, life in this world was hard and unrewarding, but the Church promised them their reward after death: 'Blessed are the meek: for they shall inherit the earth' (Matthew 5:5).

## Life and death

Life expectancy was low, especially for the working classes. Overcrowding, poor housing, lack of sanitation, no running water, low wages, poor standards of nutrition, ignorance and lack of effective medical treatment all contributed to the spread of disease. It is estimated that tuberculosis accounted for a quarter of all deaths. Other major killers were typhus, cholera and influenza, which were more or less endemic, but reached epidemic proportions frequently. Other diseases such as measles, whooping cough and diphtheria were also endemic. In Haworth, 'wool-sorter's disease', which we now know as anthrax, was virulent.

As well as disease, bad living conditions and ignorance led to food poisoning, and bad diet led to rickets, which could cause contracted pelvises, making childbirth difficult and even dangerous. Death in childbirth was not uncommon due to puerperal fever. By the age of ten years, 11% of children had lost a father, and 11% had lost a mother by the same age. Among the poor, 30% of children died before they reached their first birthday.

In Haworth, 41.6% of children died before they reached the age of six, and the average life expectancy was only 24 years. Reverend Brontë worked tirelessly to relieve the suffering of the poor, and he repeatedly petitioned the General Board of Health to improve sanitation. Eventually, when the overcrowded graveyard was contaminating the already unhealthy water supply, the Board commissioned the Babbage Report in 1850, and, as a result of this, conditions began to improve.

Reverend Brontë could not raise public subscription for the relief of the poor because the poor were regarded as an underclass whose degradation was largely their own fault. It was frequently asserted that God had made them poor, and that He wished them to remain poor. Society regarded widows, orphans, old people and the chronically sick as 'deserving' and so they could receive help through the degrading system of the Poor House. Anyone else was regarded as 'undeserving' and refused any help at all. With no unemployment benefit, no sick pay and no pensions, people needed children to support them through illness and old age, so families were large and children were sent out to work from the age of five or six.

This led to another common cause of death or crippling injury in children. Children earned only 10% of an adult wage so mill-owners liked to employ them as cheap labour. They were forced to work long hours without breaks, and tiredness and hunger frequently led to accidents with the machinery. The smallest children were employed as 'scavengers' to creep under the machines, while they were still in operation, to gather up bits of loose cotton or wool.

## 'Self-righteousness is not religion'

Established religion was used as a form of social control to keep the poor in their place and prevent them from rebelling against the establishment. At Lowood, the daughters of impoverished gentlemen are taught humility and self-sacrifice, supposedly for the good of their souls. The established Church was firmly committed to supporting the government in preserving the existing class divisions. Significantly, it was the bishops in the House of Lords who were responsible for defeating the first Reform Bill.

When the novel was criticised for being 'an insult to piety', Brontë replied in her preface to the second edition: 'Conventionality is not morality. Self-righteousness is not religion. To attack the first is not to assail the last. To pluck the mask from the face of the Pharisee is not to lift an impious hand to the Crown of Thorns…narrow human doctrines, that only tend to elate and magnify a few, should not be substituted for the world-redeeming creed of Christ.'

Charlotte Brontë would have been familiar with these 'narrow human doctrines' throughout her life. Reverend Patrick Brontë was a broad-minded and tolerant man with an optimistic and cheerful view of religion. As a theological student at Cambridge he had come under the influence of the non-conformist evangelical wing of the Anglican Church. This movement was born out of a new

sense of urgency and personal commitment to spreading the new doctrines of Christianity, and in its early days it was responsible for the reform of a number of social abuses, such as the abolition of the slave trade. However, the children's aunt, Miss Branwell, was a strict Calvinist believing in predestination and damnation, and so, even at the family dinner table, there would have been lively discussions on religious matters. The debates would have included:

- the challenge to faith posed by new scientific discoveries
- the problems posed by a more historical approach to biblical criticism
- whether God's omnipotent power and knowledge meant that he had already, before the Creation, predestined the salvation of individuals, leading to an elect few who are saved, or whether Christ died for all and so everyone is capable of being born again
- whether God had no direct involvement with the individual destinies of human beings, or whether each individual can make direct contact with God through prayer

## The danger of certainty

These religious questions are central to *Jane Eyre*. The rigidities of institutionalised religion are satirised in the inflexible Mr Brocklehurst and criticised in St John Rivers, whose sermons convey 'a strange bitterness; an absence of consolatory gentleness; stern allusions to Calvinist doctrines — election, predestination, reprobation — were frequent; and each reference to these points sounded like a sentence pronounced for doom' (Chapter XXX). St John represses his natural instinct because he is convinced that he has to choose between religion and earthly love. St John's certainty that he will win 'his incorruptible crown' leads to his early death. A religion that excludes human affections is fit for heroes, but Brontë demonstrates that it is not a creed to live by.

Nevertheless, St John is a man to be admired, but who can take Mr Brocklehurst seriously when, after his pious lecture against vanity and the lusts of the flesh, his wife and daughters enter. With well-targeted humour, Jane notes: 'They ought to have come a little sooner to have heard his lecture on dress.' Not only are they 'splendidly attired in velvet, silk, and furs', but their hair is elaborately curled and Mrs Brocklehurst even 'wore a false front of French curls'. As Jane is placed on the stool, 'a spread of shot orange and purple silk pelisses and a cloud of silvery plumage extended and waved below me' (Chapter VII). The word 'satire' comes from the same Latin root as 'saturate', and surely these three females are saturated in too much extravagant and gaudy dress.

Another devout character who dies prematurely is Helen Burns. Helen teaches Jane a 'creed which no one ever taught me', and which 'extends hope to all' (Chapter VI). She is certain that her suffering on this earth will gain its reward in heaven, and so she teaches forgiveness of one's tormentors and acceptance of one's lot. Jane is influenced by Helen's faith so that she is able to forgive Mrs Reed on her deathbed, even though she knows that this will not change her aunt's feelings for her, but she does not have Helen's absolute faith in heaven, and she cannot accept that life is merely a brief time of suffering before the better life to come.

## The prodigal son

Mr Rochester is a good example of the evangelical belief in individual regeneration. He finds faith after passing 'through the valley of the shadow of death' (Chapter XXXVII). His Byronic cynicism gives way to religious acceptance and an acknowledgement of his individual responsibility for his troubles. As soon as he turns back to God, he is rewarded because Jane hears his voice and returns to him.

Jane's own religious position is not so easy to classify. As a child she has a very pragmatic attitude that to avoid going to hell she must keep in good health and not die. A realist, she questions the very idea of heaven: 'Where is that region? Does it exist?' (Chapter IX). At Thornfield, she falls into the trap of idolatry: 'I could not, in those days, see God for His creature: of whom I had made an idol' (Chapter XXIV). As she journeys through life, her faith develops into one based on individual conscience and the guiding influence of nature. For her, the proof of God's existence is in her natural surroundings: 'We know that God is everywhere; but certainly we feel His presence most when His works are on the grandest scale spread before us; and it is in the unclouded night-sky, where His worlds wheel their silent course, that we read clearest His infinitude, His omnipotence, His omnipresence' (Chapter XXVIII).

Charlotte Brontë manages to combine the Romanticism of many of her literary influences (e.g. Wordsworth, Scott and Byron) with a strong religious faith. Jane tells St John, 'I owe to their [Diana's and Mary's] spontaneous, genuine, genial compassion as large a debt as to your evangelical charity' (Chapter XXIX). The central theme of the novel is that Jane has learned the importance of a balance between reason and feeling.

# Critical history

## Contemporary criticism

*Jane Eyre* was immediately popular, praised for its vigour and boldness, its freshness and originality, its powers of thought and expression. However, it also proved controversial. Some reviewers complained about the improbable plot and the suggestions of supernatural intervention; some were outraged by the manner in which the young Jane confronted adults, and the grown woman confronted the supposedly superior sex; some accused the writer of attacking religion in the characterisation of the hypocritical Mr Brocklehurst.

Later, when it was known to have been written by a woman, although it still sold extremely well it attracted criticism from both conservatives and radical feminists. Conservatives regarded it as politically subversive. Brontë challenged the contemporary perception of women by portraying Jane as both intelligent and passionate, equal to men in her capacity for intellectual aspiration as well as the depth of her sexual desire and the force of her anger. An autobiographical narrative necessarily asserts the importance of the individual, and expresses indignation at society's treatment of her. Conservative readers felt that God had made Jane a penniless orphan and she ought to be grateful for the charity offered by her bene-factors instead of expecting equality. In both her writing and her paintings, Jane asserts her individuality. Politically this was subversive, because if each individual is valuable in his or her own right, then each individual should have the right to vote. Britain, however, was not a democracy; only male landowners were permitted to vote. One reviewer wrote: 'We do not hesitate to say that the tone of mind and thought which has overthrown authority and violated every code, human and divine, abroad, and fostered Chartism and rebellion at home, is the same which has written *Jane Eyre*' (Elizabeth Rigby, *Quarterly Review* December 1948).

Outspoken though she is about social injustice, Charlotte Brontë was also criticised by contemporary feminists. Her friend Mary Taylor complained that she was soft on the 'rights of woman' issue. Mary had emigrated to New Zealand so that she could earn her own living in business and she felt that equal opportunity to work was an important issue that should be addressed head on. For Brontë, sentiment was more important than rights. In response to an article on the emancipation of women by John Stuart Mill, she agreed that 'if there be a natural unfitness in women for men's employment, there is no need to make laws on the subject; leave all careers open; let them try'. However, she criticises him for ignoring the heart: 'I think the writer forgets there is such a thing as self-sacrificing love and disinherited devotion' (letter to Mrs Gaskell, 20 September 1851). At the end of the novel, Brontë comes down firmly on the side of 'self-sacrificing love' as Jane suppresses her restlessness and her ambition; she marries Mr Rochester and becomes the domesticated woman she had earlier rejected.

Charlotte Brontë expressed contentment with what had been achieved for women and the change she perceived in men's attitudes to an educated woman. She felt, however, that 'there are other evils — deep-rooted in the foundation of the social system — which no efforts of ours can touch; of which we cannot complain; of which it is advisable not too often to think' (letter to Mrs Gaskell, 27 August 1850). She was not a campaigning social reformer like her friend Elizabeth Gaskell, but her novel does reflect issues and changes in her society. Schools for girls were being established and conditions were gradually improving. The social hierarchies were changing so that the son of a journeyman needlemaker, Mr Oliver, could become the most important man at Morton, while the children of the traditional gentry, Diana and Mary Rivers, have to leave home to find work. Brontë draws satirical portraits of upper-class guests at Thornfield and roundly condemns the hypocritical middle-class Mrs Reed and Mr Brocklehurst. Jane, however, expresses approval of Lowood once it is run compassionately, calling it a 'truly useful and noble institution' (Chapter X), even though its education programme is still designed to prepare the daughters of impoverished gentry for a life of duty and service.

## Modern feminist criticism

Recent feminist critics attempt to describe and interpret women's experience as depicted in literature. They question the long-standing dominant male ideologies, patriarchal attitudes and male interpretations in literature. They challenge traditional and accepted male ideas about the nature of women and how women are, according to male writers, supposed to feel, act and think. Elaine Showalter defines the period in which the Brontës were writing as the 'Feminine phase', when women first imitated a masculine tradition, followed by 'Feminist' and 'Female' phases when women protested against masculine values and traditions, and then finally advocated their own autonomous perspective (*A Literature of Their Own*, 1977). Feminist critics interpret Jane Eyre less for what Brontë advocates and more for her struggle against the cultural inhibitions by which she was conditioned. Her female protagonist, for example, could not actually express her sexual desire, so Brontë had to employ imagery. Many of the unrealistic melodramatic elements of the novel are perceived by feminist critics as evidence of Brontë's battling against the contemporary social mores and resorting to Gothic characters, events and imagery in order to suggest what she cannot express in words. Sandra M. Gilbert and Susan Gubar (1979), in their widely acclaimed study of nineteenth-century women writers *The Madwoman in the Attic*, read her forcefulness when she breaks away from St John after hearing Mr Rochester's call as:

> ...the climax of all that has gone before...The plot device of the cry is merely a sign that the relationship for which both lovers had longed is now possible, a sign that Jane's metaphoric speech of the first betrothal scene has been translated into reality 'my spirit...addresses your spirit, just as if we both had passed through the grave, and we stood at God's feet, equal — as we are!'

## Psychoanalytic criticism

Psychoanalytic critics see literature as they do dreams. Both are fictions, inventions of the mind that, although based on reality, are, by definition, not true. The theory is that much of what lies in the unconscious mind has been repressed or censored by consciousness and emerges only in disguised forms, such as dreams, or in an art form, such as painting or writing. They interpret the author's purpose in writing as being to gratify secretly some forbidden wish that has been repressed into the unconscious mind. Therefore, the novel is seen as wish-fulfilment on the part of Charlotte Brontë with its plain, poor, intelligent heroine falling madly in love with the passionate, masterful Byronic hero, but marrying him on equal terms rather than allowing herself to be dominated.

The novel is also perceived as an exploration of Jane's own repressed subconscious. Gilbert and Gubar (1979) suggest that Bertha is Jane's night-time double. Jane wants to be Mr Rochester's equal; Bertha is his equal in size and strength. Jane does not like the 'vapoury veil'; Bertha tears it in two. Jane wants to put off 'the bridal day', which she dreads as well as longs for; Bertha delays the wedding. Jane dreams of Thornfield in ruins; Bertha destroys it. 'Bertha', they conclude, 'is Jane's truest and darkest double; she is the angry aspect of the orphan child, the ferocious secret self Jane has been trying to repress ever since her days at Gateshead'.

When she decides to leave Thornfield, 'Conscience turned tyrant, held Passion by the throat', and told her 'No, you shall tear yourself away, none shall help you; you shall yourself pluck out your right eye; yourself cut off your right hand' (Chapter XXVII). This strange prophecy comes true when she marries the crippled Mr Rochester and becomes 'bone of his bone, and flesh of his flesh' (Chapter XXXVIII). It is as if her subconscious wish to be on an equal footing with Mr Rochester maims him to makes him dependent on her, removes the impediment to their marriage, and destroys Thornfield where she had been his social inferior.

## Marxist criticism

The Marxist perspective is that works of literature are conditioned by the economic and political forces of their social context. Not only is Charlotte Brontë advocating the rights of the individual and universal education, but the whole plot of the novel is dictated by the need to create equality between a penniless orphan who arrives at Thornfield as a servant and her wealthy and dominant employer. She has to leave Thornfield and achieve independence; he has to become weaker and more dependent. Only when social conventions have been observed can they come together as equals and achieve a fulfilling and loving relationship. In *Myths of Power*, Terry Eagleton reads Charlotte Brontë's novels as 'myths which work towards a balance or fusion of blunt bourgeois rationality and flamboyant Romanticism, brash initiative and genteel cultivation, passionate rebellion and cautious conformity'. It is the tensions between these opposites that give *Jane Eyre* its dramatic power and lasting appeal.

## Post-colonial criticism

Post-colonial critics oppose the view that 'culture' refers exclusively to 'high' culture and place a great deal of emphasis on the practice of everyday life. They focus on culture in relation to ideologies, which are different ways of viewing the world held by classes or individuals who have power in a given social group. Post-colonial critics have explored *Jane Eyre* in the context of the British Empire and the patronising attitudes of the dominant Christian English society to British colonies. Briggs's letter states that Bertha's mother is a 'creole', which could mean either that she is of European descent, or that she is of mixed race. In either case, Bertha might have evoked British anxieties about having to deal with the other cultures under British dominion, and Bertha's imprisonment might signify Britain's attempts to control and contain the influences of these subject cultures. Rochester's marriage to Bertha represents the British Empire's cultural and economic exploitation of its colonial subjects. It is significant that Edward Rochester's wealth was made on the backs of slaves in the West Indies, a fact which Jean Rhys makes explicit in *Wide Sargasso Sea*, a prequel to *Jane Eyre*. St John Rivers goes as a missionary to India, with arrogant hopes 'of carrying knowledge into the realms of ignorance — of substituting…religion for superstition', which is another way of exercising control (Chapter XXXII).

## Deconstruction

To deconstruct a text is to show that it can have interpretations that are opposites and yet intertwined. Terry Eagleton (1975) points out the broad opposites that intertwine in the novel. Brontë, for instance, gives us the perspective of the child, Jane Eyre, so we learn how she felt at the time, as well as the interpretation of the adult, Jane Rochester, who is telling her story. Mr Rochester thinks his marriage to Bertha Mason destroyed him, but the reader can see that it gave him financial independence and social position. Jane is a modern woman, ambitious, independent, passionate, but at the same time she is trapped in nineteenth-century thinking, and to us she appears intellectually as well as socially snobbish. She knows, for instance, that she should not have feelings of dismay and degradation about teaching at the village school, but Brontë uses the future tense when she asserts 'I shall get the better of them', indicating that she has not yet conquered her feelings of 'disgust' at 'the ignorance, the poverty, the coarseness' (Chapter XXXI).

# Literary background

# Fictional autobiography

Compared with the other broad categories of drama, poetry and non-fiction, the novel is a recent literary genre. Its beginnings can be traced back to the sixteenth century, when people started writing prose narratives. In the seventeenth century, after the Restoration, authors such as Aphra Behn, John Bunyan and Daniel Defoe wrote books we can term 'proto-novels', which have a story rather than a plot, relating a sequence of events with little development in the central characters. It was not until the eighteenth century that true novels emerged. By this time, the form had been developed so that, instead of a series of events being narrated chronologically, writers constructed a plot that linked events together, exploring cause and effect, revealing significances and reaching a planned conclusion.

The genre grew in popularity with the expansion of the middle class, because the daughters of tradesmen were better educated than their parents, but they were not permitted to work or study for a career like their husbands and brothers. Like the wives and daughters of the landed gentry and the professional class, they had servants to do most of the housework, so there was a growing number of women with plenty of leisure time. Circulating libraries started up to make it possible for people to read more books than they could afford to buy and to satisfy the great demand for entertaining fiction.

## Memoir-novels

At the beginning of the eighteenth century, a new form of novel, fictional auto-biography or 'memoir-novels', became popular. The first well-known memoir-novel is *Robinson Crusoe*, which was published in 1719. In this book Daniel Defoe created an impression of realism by adapting Puritan self-confession narratives to suit the mode of a fictional moral tract. Crusoe relates his fall from grace as he defies his parents and runs away to sea, then the bulk of the novel traces his slow, painful journey back to a state of grace. Crusoe is an educated man from a 'good family' so he narrates his experiences and achievements meticulously, because he is recording the nature of his moral survival and redemption.

Seven years later, Jonathan Swift published the more complex *Gulliver's Travels*, for which he created another reliable narrator. As a surgeon, Lemuel Gulliver is well educated and informed, not only professionally but also politically. His travels take him to extraordinary and fantastic societies, which he observes closely, and he records the details of his experiences scrupulously, as is expected from a medical practitioner. However, as his name implies, he is easily 'gulled' and seems oblivious to the parallels with his own society, which Swift's satire is intended to ridicule. Brontë writes in Chapter III that, as a child, Jane 'considered it a narrative of facts' and 'doubted not that [she] might one day, by taking a long voyage, see with [her] own eyes the little fields, houses, and trees, the diminutive people, the tiny cows, sheep, and birds of the one realm; and the cornfields forest-high, the mighty mastiffs, the monster cats, the tower-like men and women of the other'.

## Epistolary novels

It was not until Samuel Richardson, in the 1740s, that novels with first-person narratives achieved the moral introspection and psychological insight that characterises *Jane Eyre*. In his epistolary novel, *Clarissa*, Richardson weaves together four main narrative voices, supported by various minor characters of differing age, class, and point of view, to construct a novel of great psychological complexity. Another highly popular epistolary novel was Jean-Jacques Rousseau's *Julie, ou la Nouvelle Héloïse* in which a critical account of contemporary manners and ideas is interwoven with a passionate love story. In 1818, Mary Shelley used letters as the framework for her novel *Frankenstein*, which juxtaposes the supposed narratives of the eponymous scientist and his creation.

# Romanticism

When people say that Charlotte Brontë was influenced by Romantic writers, they are not merely referring to the fact that *Jane Eyre* is a love story about a poor Cinderella figure who ends up married to the man she adores. The Romantic period refers to a movement in the arts and ways of thinking that pervaded Europe at the end of the eighteenth century and the beginning of the nineteenth. Many writers, artists and musicians reacted against the neo-Classical Age of Reason that characterised eighteenth-century thought. Instead of prizing reason and logical thinking, the new thinkers insisted that the emotional side of human responses was more important, that the brain should learn from the heart and natural instinct, and that the imagination held purer truths than the mind. Nature was all important, and some writers even rejected established religion and worshipped nature instead. In place of the eighteenth-century fascination with all things classical, writers and painters turned to the medieval, the Gothic, the foreign, the exotic, and the supernatural.

## Reason versus Nature

Charlotte Brontë read widely among the Romantics and it is easy to see their influence in *Jane Eyre*. Jane values reason, and indeed it dictates her behaviour when she leaves Thornfield, but love is more important to her, and when she has to choose between a man she admires who declares 'Reason, and not feeling, is my guide' (Chapter XXXII) and the man she loves, who has a 'resistless *bent* to love faithfully and well' (Chapter XXVII), she realises that she needs love more than intellectual challenges. Jane is strongly influenced by nature, and looks there first for protection and guidance. When she flees from Thornfield, she declares: 'I have no relative but the universal mother, Nature: I will seek her breast and ask repose' (Chapter XXVIII). She finds somewhere sheltered to sleep and some berries to eat, and only then does she say her 'evening prayers', as if by routine rather than need. Not until nightfall does she feel 'the might and strength of God'.

A love of nature is what Jane and Mr Rochester have in common. In the final chapter, she gives no details of what she has been reading to her blind husband, but she does list how she puts 'into words the effect of field, tree, town, river, cloud, sunbeam — of the landscape before us, of the weather around us'. Settings are very important in the novel, and Jane often uses natural imagery as a means of explaining her feelings. After the revelation that Mr Rochester has a wife, she feels as if winter has come: 'A Christmas frost' (Chapter XVI).

It is the fact that Mr Rochester is already married, rather than his wife's madness, that is essential for the plot. However, this device allows Brontë to introduce many Romantic elements. Thornfield has battlements, like a medieval castle. Bertha herself is described as a monster or demon. She comes from the West Indies, an exotic place where English reserve and decorum may not be so valued. To escape her, Rochester has travelled widely in Europe and has had a succession of foreign mistresses. In the midst of all this Gothic horror and foreignness, the central figure of Jane seems to embody English reserve, self-restraint and Quakerish plainness.

## Marriage

Unlike the Romantic writers, Charlotte Brontë does not condone illicit love, but makes Jane think rationally that:

> ...if I were so far to forget myself and all the teaching that had ever been instilled into me, as — under any pretext — with any justification — through any temptation — to become the successor of these poor girls, he would one day regard me with the same feeling which now in his mind desecrated their memory. (Chapter XXVII)

Jane does not live for the moment nor succumb to her feelings; she overcomes them and is rewarded. She trusts in God and her own self-respect. Brontë respects the institution of marriage, even as she recognises its drawbacks. If Jane had married St John Rivers, she would have lost her precious independence. As his companion:

> ...my heart and mind would be free. I should still have my unblighted self to turn to: my natural unenslaved feelings with which to communicate in moments of loneliness. There would be recesses in my mind which would be only mine, to which he never came; and sentiments there fresh and sheltered. (Chapter XXXIV)

## Social reform

The emphasis on the importance of the individual is to be found in all Romantic writers. Inspired by the revolution in America, with its declaration of human rights, the French revolutionary cry of *Liberté, Egalité, Fraternité*, and by the abolition of the slave trade, people began to argue for reform in England. Romantic thinkers argued not just for freedom for themselves but also for reforms in society. Although Brontë graphically describes the lives of governesses and the hardships faced by children in charity schools, she does not advocate reform.

Rosamond Oliver is the one character in the book who is a social reformer, bringing education to the village children, including girls. She, however, is dismissed by Jane as 'not profoundly interesting or thoroughly impressive' and 'a sweet girl — rather thoughtless' (Chapter XXXII). It seems ironic to a twenty-first century reader that Jane, who thinks only of herself, despising the 'heavy-looking gaping rustics' (Chapter XXXII) she has to teach, and feeling 'degraded' by taking 'a step which sank instead of raising me in the scale of social existence' (Chapter XXXI), is so dismissive of the young woman who actively embraces social reform, spending much of her allowance on tackling their ignorance and sharing some of the teaching herself. When married, Jane apparently does nothing for anyone other than her immediate family, applauding herself for finding a more indulgent school for Adèle.

# The Pilgrim's Progress

Brontë makes several references to this allegorical novel written by John Bunyan in the seventeenth century. Through the device of a dream, Bunyan tells how its hero, Christian, journeys from the City of Destruction to the Celestial City. His journey is beset by troubles, represented by images such as the Slough of Despond, the Castle of Giant Despair, and the Valley of the Shadow of Death. He meets various characters with appropriate names, both helpful and destructive, along the way. In her references to Bunyan's work, Brontë invites her readers to read the novel, on one level, as a mythic quest. Jane struggles from the imprisonment of her childhood towards independence and equality. Like all women in a patriarchal society, she must meet and overcome oppression at Gateshead, humiliation at Lowood, temptation of the flesh at Thornfield and temptation of the spirit at Marsh End. Instead of making her story overtly allegorical, like Bunyan, Brontë adopts the form of a *Bildungsroman*, i.e an account of the youthful development of a hero or heroine. It uses a realistic framework to describe the various ups and downs from which the character achieves self-knowledge.

It is, however, worth noting the echoes of, and direct references to, *The Pilgrim's Progress*. After her furious outburst at Mrs Reed, Jane learns that: 'A child…cannot give its furious feelings uncontrolled play, as I had given mine — without experiencing afterwards the pang of remorse and the chill of reaction.' She stands in the garden, whispering the words of Bunyan's Christian over and over again: '"What shall I do? — What shall I do?"' (Chapter IV). Later, when she saves Mr Rochester from the fire, she is unable to sleep. 'Till morning dawned I was tossed on a buoyant but unquiet sea, where billows of trouble rolled under surges of joy. I thought sometimes I saw beyond its wild waters a shore, sweet as the hills of Beulah' (Chapter XV). Bunyan tells his readers that, in the Land of Beulah, 'the sun shineth night and day'. Jane, however, resists the temptation to think her employer might fall in love with her.

After her hopes of marriage are shattered, Charlotte Brontë uses an allegorical technique as Jane personifies elements of her personality. 'Conscience' told 'Passion' that 'she had yet but dipped her dainty foot in the slough, and swore that with that arm of iron he would thrust her down to unsounded depths of agony' (Chapter XXVII). Unlike Christian, however, she meets no 'Help' to save her from the 'Slough of Despond', and she has to tear herself away. Alone on the moor, she muses: 'Life, however, was yet in my possession, with all its requirements, and pains, and responsibilities. The burden must be carried' (Chapter XXVIII). It was 'the burden that was upon his back' that prevented Christian from extricating himself from the Slough, but the burden fell away when he saw the cross and the sepulchre. Significantly, Jane hears a church bell, but she does not go into the church. The Celestial City is the goal of those who accept the Church's teaching that we suffer in this life but will gain our reward in the next. It is not Jane's goal. After conquering her despair, Jane collapses at the door of Marsh House when Hannah refuses her entry: 'Not only the anchor of hope, but the footing of fortitude was gone — at least for the moment: but the last I soon endeavoured to regain.' She is lifted up by St John, just as Mercy was lifted up by the keeper of the wicket gate after struggling through the Slough of Despond in the second part of *The Pilgrim's Progress*.

St John tempts her to sacrifice herself on the altar of religion, but she hears Mr Rochester's voice and is convinced that this is the work of Nature, telling her that it was her time 'to assume ascendancy. *My* powers were in play, and in force' (Chapter XXXV). This is the end of Jane's journey: she has won through to a life that is 'supremely blest — blest beyond what language can express' (Chapter XXXVIII). Brontë reminds us again of Bunyan's *Pilgrim's Progress,* however, at the very end of the novel, when St John faces death eagerly, anticipating 'his sure reward, his incorruptible crown'. He has devoted his life to guiding others to the Celestial City, like the warrior Great-heart, 'who guards his pilgrim convoy from the onslaughts of Apollyon'.

# Gothic fiction

Writers have always exploited the way in which readers or theatre-goers enjoy the thrill of being scared. The success of Shakespeare's *Macbeth,* as just one example, is due in large part to the supernatural intervention of the three witches. *Beowulf* would probably not have delighted listeners and readers for more than a millennium if the composer had not introduced terrifying monsters to threaten the harmony of the mead-hall. In the middle of the eighteenth century, Horace Walpole initiated a craze for these thrills in novels. He called his book *The Castle of Otranto: A Gothic Story*. In using the word 'Gothic', he was evoking an ancient Germanic tribe from the so-called 'Dark Ages' that lost its ethnic identity in the sixth century. Gothic fiction, in whatever medium, works by introducing the unfamiliar, the inexplicable, the irrational, into a familiar, safe and realistic world. They are tales of mystery and fear, designed to chill the spine and curdle the blood, but only enough to evoke a delightful horror.

The earliest stories featured a beautiful young woman who would be abducted and threatened with seduction, or worse. The plot would move from the secure comfort of the parental home to the menacing environment of the abductor's abode. This would typically be an isolated, medieval castle with locked doors, dark corners and mysterious happenings. The helpless heroine would eventually be saved by the handsome, safe, young man who loves her. Many Gothic novels were written by women and they have been seen to represent a young woman's fear of marriage. In the eighteenth century, marriage for the educated, novel-reading class was often a business arrangement. Even if the young lady were lucky enough to marry for love, she would be chaperoned throughout the courtship and so have no opportunity to get to know her husband before the wedding. Her apprehension about married life and her future spouse were therefore quite understandable, as was her ignorant fear of the wedding night.

## Sophisticated Gothic

By the nineteenth century, the appeal of the conventional Gothic horror novel was beginning to wane, and novelists were using its stock ingredients in more sophisticated ways. It is easy to recognise Brontë's debt to the genre, but she blends its elements with a realism that gently mocks the overactive imagination of her heroine. Jane Austen's *Northanger Abbey* was a model for this treatment. Jane compares the corridor of the third storey of Thornfield with Bluebeard's castle, evoking Charles Perrault's fairy tale in which Bluebeard's young wife finds the corpses of his previous wives hanging on the walls of a locked room. Mr Rochester is no murderer, however, and, in fact, it was common practice for a woman to be locked up if her husband decided she was mad. (See the novella *The Yellow Wallpaper* by Charlotte Perkins Gilman.) 'The foul German spectre — the vampire', who tears Jane's veil is, in reality, his unhappy first wife (Chapter XXV).

When Jane hears Mr Rochester's horse approaching, she thinks of the Gytrash, 'a North-of-England spirit' which 'sometimes came upon belated travellers'. The huge dog that appears out of the gloom appears 'exactly one mask of Bessie's Gytrash — a lion-like creature with long hair and a huge head' (Chapter XII). Brontë, however, undermines Jane's fanciful imaginings with humour. The 'Gytrash' is Pilot, a friendly dog who wags his tail at Jane; the Byronic hero, far from being 'mad, bad, and dangerous to know', falls from his horse and needs Jane's help to remount. When his bed is set on fire to the accompaniment of a 'demoniac laugh' and 'goblin-laughter', Brontë dispels the Gothic atmosphere as Mr Rochester wakes 'fulminating strange anathemas at finding himself lying in a pool of water' (Chapter XV). In appearance, Mr Rochester is a typical Gothic hero, dark and brooding. He has a domineering manner, an aggressive contempt for convention and has travelled widely. He is, however, vulnerable. He has a strong feeling of responsibility for his first wife and was reluctant to commit bigamy, preparing to do so only because he had become convinced that Jane would refuse to live with him as his mistress.

Brontë deviates from the conventional Gothic novel again in St John Rivers. At first, apparently, the young, handsome and devout hero who saves the heroine, the reader eventually realises that he is more dangerous than Mr Rochester. Instead of making him the safe 'boy-next-door', Brontë has drawn out his piety to a threatening extreme so that Jane declares: 'If I were to marry you, you would kill me. You are killing me now' (Chapter XXXV). This appears a melodramatic accusation, but Jane reflects the prejudice of her time in truly believing that she would die if she went to India. Jane herself, of course, is neither beautiful, nor a helpless victim.

## The supernatural

Gothic fiction was designed to intensify the reader's emotional response by bringing elements of horror into a romantic novel. Brontë intensifies our response even more successfully by combining Gothic elements with a rational realism. The supernatural references are mostly metaphorical as Bertha is compared with a 'goblin' or 'vampire', and Jane is accused of being a 'witch', a 'sprite' or an 'elf'. When she does introduce supernatural elements, like the white human form who advises her to 'flee temptation', it is usually in a dream.

The one event that is difficult to explain rationally is the moment of telepathy when Jane and Mr Rochester hear each other's voices. Jane, however, tries to explain it rationally, rejecting superstition and comparing the sensation with an electric shock, as if it is, in reality, the moment when she realises 'It was *my* time to assume ascendancy. *My* powers were in play and in force' (Chapter XXXV). For Mr Rochester, hearing Jane's voice appears to be his reward for eventually turning to God and beginning to pray. It seems that although Brontë does use a supernatural event, she does so to reinforce her main themes rather than contribute to the horror.

# Chapter summaries and notes

## Chapter I

Brontë starts Jane's fictional autobiography with the first time she rebels against injustice and male oppression, fighting back when John Reed bullies her. From the beginning Jane is established as an outsider, excluded from the Reed family group.

- Bewick's *History of British Birds* was one of Brontë's favourite books as a child. It is illustrated with many imaginative scenes, or vignettes, which she used to copy.
- The adult Jane also quotes from James Thompson's *The Seasons*, and she refers to novels by Samuel Richardson (*Pamela*) and Henry Brooke (*Henry Earl of Moreland*).
- Note how Brontë introduces the recurring psychological symbols of fire and ice.

## Chapter II

Jane is locked in the red-room, where Mr Reed died, as punishment for her behaviour, which is interpreted as evidence that she is out of control. Miss Abbott declares her less than a servant. She grows frightened and screams, but is locked in again. She loses consciousness.

- Like the window-seat where she sought refuge, the red-room has folds of scarlet drapery and is an enclosed space that symbolises Jane's private, internal world, but here she is trapped and vulnerable to her overactive imagination.
- The 'tabernacle' was the curtained tent that housed the Jewish Ark of the Covenant, but is also used to refer to an ornate, canopied structure that houses a tomb. Its use helps to explain why Jane is overcome with awe.

## Chapter III

Jane wakes in the nursery, where the apothecary has been called to treat her. She tells her story for the first time when she tries to explain to Mr Lloyd why she is miserable. He suggests that she might like to go to school.

- An 'apothecary' is not a fully qualified doctor, and so his services are less expensive. Mrs Reed would have employed a doctor for her own children.
- *Gulliver's Travels* was a popular but dark satire by Jonathan Swift, the first two books of which can be read as children's stories about pygmies and giants. Charlotte Brontë marks the start of Jane's growth to maturity by showing her changed perception of a book that had been a source of delight but is now full of dread and desolation.
- Bessie sings an unknown ballad that is thought to have been written by Charlotte Brontë. It foreshadows what will happen to Jane when she is lost and alone on the moors, and it sums up an important theme of the novel — the search for a home. Significantly, the popular view of God is that he is a 'friend to the poor orphan child'.
- Guy Fawkes was one of the notorious Catholic conspirators who plotted to blow up the Houses of Parliament. The adult Jane seems amused that Miss Abbott thought of her as a dangerous anarchist. He is clearly introduced because of his association with fire and explosiveness.

## Chapter IV

Mr Brocklehurst comes to inspect Jane, and his hypocritical account of Lowood Institution reveals that it is designed to prepare the daughters of impoverished gentlemen for their subservient position in society. Jane is deeply hurt when Mrs Reed tells him Jane is deceitful and, after he has left, accuses her fiercely of injustice and cruelty. Jane has learned to stand up for herself but, although triumphant at her victory, vengeance leaves a sour taste.

- *The Child's Guide* was an evangelical magazine, edited by Reverend Carus Wilson, who founded the Clergy Daughters' School at Cowan Bridge, which Charlotte Brontë blamed for the deaths of her elder sisters.

## Chapter V

Jane clings to Bessie and has to be torn from her to be put in the coach to Lowood. We are given details of the harsh discipline at Lowood. The poor food and the uniforms that give the girls no protection from the cold, are designed to prevent them from blossoming into young women, and the emphasis on religion hypocritically implies that their suffering is for the good of their souls. Jane meets Helen Burns, who explains about the supposedly 'charitable' institution.

- 'stony street' is a quotation from Byron's *Childe Harold*. Charlotte admired Lord Byron's poetry and recommended her friend, Ellen Nussey, to read it. She advised her not to read *Don Juan,* although she had read and enjoyed the epic poem.
- When Jane speaks of her 'organ of veneration', she is referring to the pseudo-science of phrenology, popular in the nineteenth century, in which various parts of the head were thought to be responsible for personal qualities.
- The irony of the inscription lauding Mrs Brocklehurst's 'good works' is underlined by the sound of Helen's cough; she will soon die from the tuberculosis which the privations at Lowood have done much to exacerbate.
- *Rasselas* is a didactic romance about the aims of human life, in which Samuel Johnson philosophises about the vanity of this world. Helen is clearly highly intelligent and very serious.

## Chapter VI

Jane observes Helen being victimised again, even though she is the only girl in the class who can answer Miss Scatcherd's questions. Jane feels unavailing and impotent anger, but Helen reveals no emotion. Helen tries to teach her the New Testament values of endurance, forgiveness and turning the other cheek.

- 'Tonnage', 'poundage' and 'ship-money' were taxes illegally imposed by King Charles I, which led to the English Civil War and the King's execution by parliament. Through this topic, Charlotte Brontë raises the question of whether rebellion is ever justifiable.

## Chapter VII

Mr Brocklehurst inspects the school and explains his policies to reject what is natural as dangerous and bad; nature is to be crushed as part of the girls' training. He declares Jane to be a liar and humiliates her in front of the whole school, but Helen gives her an inspirational look.

- Ironically, the régime at Lowood does not foster Christian values but promotes bullying, as the bigger girls hog the fire and steal food from the younger girls.
- Charlotte Brontë's choice of the 'fifth, sixth and seventh chapters of St Matthew' is ironic as they contain the Sermon on the Mount, which is mostly concerned with the promise of reward in heaven for those who have suffered on earth.
- Mr Brocklehurst believes in predestination and tells everyone that Jane is a 'castaway', meaning that she is beyond salvation, already claimed by the devil.

■ He says that Jane is worse than a believer in 'Juggernaut', which is the idol of the divinity of the Hindu God, Krishna. Worshippers were wrongly believed by Europeans to throw themselves under the wheels of the vehicle carrying the statue in procession and be crushed to death.

## Chapter VIII

After her ordeal, Jane wished to die because of the humiliation. Helen reassures her, and Miss Temple invites them both to her room. She tells Miss Temple her story in a restrained manner. The superintendent writes for confirmation to Mr Lloyd. Jane's name is publicly cleared; she works hard and is promoted to a higher class.

■ This is a significant moment in Jane's development, as she has learned to arrange her story coherently.

■ Helen seems to have been based on Charlotte's eldest sister, Maria, who contracted tuberculosis at school and died.

## Chapter IX

As Jane flourishes at Lowood, the weather improves and she is given more freedom. However, she reveals that the reason for this is that there is a serious outbreak of typhus and many of the girls die. Jane suddenly realises that Helen, who has consumption (tuberculosis), is seriously ill and is determined to see her. Helen is looking forward to death as a blessed release from suffering, but Jane questions whether heaven exists.

■ Charlotte Brontë repeats the same point: 'it entered my mind as it had never done before', 'my mind made its first earnest effort', 'for the first time', 'for the first time' (p. 94). This is an important turning point for Jane, when she begins to understand the meaning of death.

■ Brontë writes of 'fog-bred pestilence' because bacteria had not yet been discovered, so nineteenth-century medicine thought that the 'effluvia of mortality' rose out of the bowels of the earth.

■ 'Resurgam' is Latin for 'I shall rise again.' The word encapsulates Helen's belief in heaven and a benevolent God.

## Chapter X

Jane Rochester summarises the eight years following Helen's death. The outbreak of typhus led to an enquiry and the school was reformed. Jane works hard, gaining an excellent education, and eventually becomes a teacher. When Miss Temple leaves to get married, Lowood no longer feels like home and Jane is restless, so she advertises and accepts a position as governess. Bessie visits her, declares that she looks like a lady, and tells her about a visit from Jane's uncle, Mr Eyre of Madeira, seven years earlier.

- The blue peaks on the horizon, which Jane longs to surmount, symbolise her aspirations. This is one of the points in the novel that outraged Charlotte Brontë's critics at the time of publication because Victorian women were not supposed to extend their horizons beyond home and duty.

## Chapter XI

Jane arrives at Thornfield late at night, and her apprehensions are dispelled by a warm welcome from Mrs Fairfax. The next day she meets Adèle and learns about the absent master of the house. She is shown round the house. The possibility of some horrible secret, aroused by a tragic and preternatural laugh, is dispelled by the appearance of Grace Poole.

- There is irony in Jane's play on the name of the house: 'My couch had no thorns in it that night'.
- Like the red-room at Gateshead, Mr Rochester's drawing room is 'furnished with a general blending of snow and fire', so Charlotte Brontë reminds us of past terrors and hints at terrors to come.
- In the fairy story, Bluebeard allows his young wife to open any door she likes, except one. Curious, she enters the forbidden room and finds the bodies of his previous wives. Jane has been reading Gothic horror novels and is looking for adventure.

## Chapter XII

After three pleasant months at Thornfield, Jane is once again restless, feeling that she is stagnating. On the way to post a letter in Hay, she stops to watch a dramatic sunset. Hearing the clatter of hooves, she remembers Bessie's stories about the legendary Gytrash, but the illusion is dispelled when a man appears on a horse, which slips on the ice and falls. Having helped him to remount, she is left feeling disturbed, and unwilling to enter the house and return to the 'fetters' of the unchanging pleasantness of her life. She recognises Mr Rochester's dog on her return.

- Charlotte Brontë politicises women's rights, placing Jane's claim for equality with men in the context of 'political rebellions', revealing a strong awareness of the unrest among working people. This was thought very dangerous by some contemporary reviewers.
- The strange laugh is heard while Jane is feeling thus frustrated, supporting Gilbert and Gubar's suggestion that Bertha represents Jane's alter ego, her passionate self (*The Madwoman in the Attic*).
- Brontë personifies the moon 'seeming to look up as she left the hill-tops'. The moon is often present at key moments in her life, and she is 'not at all afraid of being out late when it is moonlight'.

## Chapter XIII

The following evening, Jane and Adèle are invited to join Mr Rochester. Jane studies his features by the light of the fire, observing the qualities of decisiveness and a hasty temper. He interrogates her about her time at Lowood, scrutinising three paintings and then dismissing her abruptly. Mrs Fairfax gives Jane a brief and incomplete summary of Mr Rochester's troubles.

- In the first of many such references, Mr Rochester links Jane with the spirit world, accusing her of bewitching his horse and spreading ice on the causeway.
- Jane answers evasively when he questions her about her relatives: 'none that I ever saw.' Misleading him like this encourages him later to ask her to marry him, thinking she has no relatives to interfere.
- The first painting owes its setting to Bewick's *History of British Birds*, but it has been painted in the style of John Martin, and the subject is reminiscent of his *Assuaging the Waters*. In Milton's *Paradise Lost,* the cormorant is a symbol of temptation and deception. The drowned girl foreshadows Jane's quotation from the Psalms at the end of Chapter XXVI.
- The second painting depicts the mountain of Latmos where, according to Greek mythology, Selene, goddess of the moon, first saw and fell in love with Endymion, vowing to protect him for evermore. The Evening Star is the planet Venus, goddess of love. It suggests Jane's longing for love, and it foreshadows Bertha, standing on the battlements before she jumps.
- The third painting also owes its setting to Bewick. 'The likeness of a kingly crown;' and 'the shape which shape had none' are quotations from Milton's *Paradise Lost* and they refer to Death, who is one of the keepers guarding the gates of hell, preventing Satan and the other fallen angels from leaving.
- In these pictures, which Jane painted at Lowood, Charlotte Brontë reveals her inner feelings of despair, her preoccupation with death, and her longing for love. However, she also foreshadows later scenes in the novel.

## Chapter XIV

Some days later, Jane and Adèle are summoned again. Mr Rochester tries to bully her, but she proves a match for him and he clearly admires this. He recognises the restlessness in Jane's nature and for the first time compares her with a bird, trapped in a cage.

- Charlotte Brontë poignantly uses the past tense as Jane Rochester writes: 'he had great, dark eyes'.
- Rochester warns her to 'Dread remorse when you are tempted to err'. Ironically, it will be he who tempts her to 'err' by begging her to stay when she knows he is married.
- When he declares 'I have a right to get pleasure out of life; and I *will* get it, cost what it may', Brontë suggests that this is the point at which he decides that he will try to make Jane fall in love with him.
- In a first-person narrative, it is difficult for the writer to give the inner feelings of other characters. Brontë successfully suggests that Mr Rochester is battling with his conscience, while still preserving the mystery, because Jane writes only what she felt at the time.

## Chapter XV

Mr Rochester meets Jane in the grounds and tells her about his liaison with Céline Varens, Adèle's mother. We realise that Jane is falling in love with him, and that night she hears strange noises, finds his bed on fire and douses the flames. Charlotte Brontë gives hints that he is in love with her.

- Contemporary critics were scandalised that a man tells an unmarried woman about his love affair, and even more that Jane entered a gentleman's bedroom.
- In the final paragraph, Charlotte Brontë is referring to Bunyan's *The Pilgrim's Progress* where Beulah is the pleasant land beyond the Valley of the Shadow of Death and out of sight of Doubting Castle. 'Beulah' in Hebrew means married. However, 'even in fancy' Jane is unable to reach it: 'Sense would resist delirium; judgment would warn passion.' Thus later events are foreshadowed.

## Chapter XVI

Mr Rochester departs suddenly. Mrs Fairfax and Adèle notice that Jane is flushed and feverish. Jane suspects Grace Poole of starting the fire and of having some secret hold over him, possibly having been his mistress. Grace Poole warns her to lock her door at night. Mrs Fairfax tells Jane about Blanche Ingram and Jane suspects that Mr Rochester is planning to marry her. She warns herself of the danger of letting a secret love kindle within her.

## Chapter XVII

Mr Rochester writes that he is inviting guests, so extra servants are brought in and the house prepared. Gossiping servants fall silent as Jane approaches. The guests arrive, and Jane's presence is required after dinner. She secretes herself in the window seat, from where she observes the guests and the entrance of Mr Rochester. She notes: 'He made me love him without looking at me.' Mr Rochester encourages his guests to speak disparagingly about governesses. He sings a Corsair song, accompanied by Blanche, and Jane slips out. He follows her and insists that she attends every evening.

- We are reminded that Jane is an unreliable narrator when she blames the coffee for the 'fiery glow' that suddenly rose to her face when Mr Rochester's letter arrives.
- Charlotte Brontë takes advantage of Jane's ambivalent position to have her present but not included, so that she can give a satirical portrayal of the upper-class guests.
- As the gentlemen enter, Brontë reverts to the present tense so that we can feel Jane's spontaneous reactions to Mr Rochester's arrival.
- Lord Byron's corsair is one of the Byronic heroes that influenced Brontë in her presentation of Mr Rochester.

## Chapter XVIII

The house party has a game of charades, and Jane is convinced that her master will marry Blanche. Later, Mr Rochester departs on business, and a stranger, Mr Mason, calls. An old gypsy woman appears and insists on telling the fortunes of the young, single ladies.

- In the charades, Mr Rochester's first role is as Blanche's bridegroom, a role presumably designed to arouse Jane's jealousy, but one that foreshadows the mock marriage he will put Jane through.
- In his second role, he is dressed as an Eastern emir, foreshadowing the way Jane feels that he behaves towards her during their engagement, like a sultan to a favoured slave. As Eliezer tempting Rebekah to marry Isaac by proffering jewels, it offers an unfavourable comment on the way he is playing with Blanche's hopes.
- In the third role he is dressed as a desperate prisoner in Bridewell. This suggests his marital status, chained to a mad wife, and it also foreshadows when Jane first sees him at Ferndean and describes him as like 'some wronged and fettered wild beast or bird'.
- Note the satirical sketch of the Ladies Lynn and Ingram as 'a pair of magnified puppets' with which Brontë neatly punctures their pretentiousness.
- The guests praise Mr Mason's appearance, but Jane is repelled by him, describing him in a series of negatives: his eye had 'no meaning in its wandering', there was 'no power…no firmness…no thought…no command…'. Brontë may be preparing us for meeting Bertha, his sister, and learning her story.

## Chapter XIX

Through his subterfuge of dressing as a gypsy, Mr Rochester is able to read Jane's face by the light of the fire, confirming that she is passionate, but that she will not give in to her feelings if they go against her conscience. He tries to lead Jane to reveal her feelings, but she is very guarded in her replies. When he drops his disguise, she tells him of Mr Mason's arrival. He grips her hand convulsively and staggers; once again he leans on her for support. She now admits to him: 'I'd give my life to serve you.'

- Once again, Brontë uses the image of flames to represent the sexual quality of Jane and Mr Rochester's relationship. Jane backs away saying 'the fire scorches me'.

## Chapter XX

The moon wakes Jane, who hears a horrifying scream, followed by a struggle and cries for help. She observes the guests' consternation, dresses herself and waits in her room. The guests pacified, Mr Rochester asks Jane to follow him to the attic where Mr Mason lies bleeding. Mr Rochester forbids them to speak and leaves Jane as nurse while he goes for the doctor. As dawn approaches, they return, and the doctor finds that Mr Mason has been bitten as well as stabbed. The doctor and Mr Mason depart. Mr Rochester and Jane talk as the sun rises. The mystery deepens as he gives more hints about his past and talks of reformation through a stranger. Jane promises to obey him 'in all that is right'. He suddenly starts talking of marriage to Blanche.

- Note the way Brontë juxtaposes a satirical sketch of the upper-class house guests with the Gothic horror of the mysterious attack. Even the high-ranking officer, Colonel Dent, whom one might reasonably expect to take command of the situation, is bemoaning that he cannot find Mr Rochester. Brontë creates an amusing cartoon with a neat simile when the two dowagers, 'like ships in full sail', bear down on their host who is being almost strangled by the clinging Misses Eshton.
- 'She sucked the blood': Bertha is associated with a vampire, a re-animated corpse that feeds on the blood of the living.
- 'your sun at noon darkens in an eclipse': this image was used as a metaphor for blindness by John Milton in *Samson Agonistes*. It is one of several references that link Mr Rochester to Samson, who lost his immense strength when he was betrayed by a woman and then blinded.

## Chapter XXI

Jane dreams of a baby every night for a week and fears it is an ill omen. Her cousin John has squandered the family fortune and eventually committed suicide. Her dying aunt summons her to Gateshead to give Jane a three-year old letter from her uncle, whom she told that Jane died at Lowood.

- Brontë often uses Jane's sensitivity to presentiments, sympathies and signs to foreshadow coming events and create suspense.
- Jane has matured from the child who declared that she would never forgive her aunt.
- Significantly, Jane thinks of Helen Burns and 'her faith — her doctrine of the equality of disembodied souls', thus admitting that she does not believe it herself.
- Mrs Reed addresses Jane with the second person pronoun 'you' and then changes to the third person as she talks to herself about Jane: 'I had better tell her'. This suggests a distancing through shame. After Jane reads the letter, Mrs Reed reverts to the second person.
- It is ironic that Mrs Reed accused Jane of lying and now dies troubled by the lie she told Mr Eyre of Madeira.

## Chapter XXII

After a month away, Jane returns to Thornfield. Mrs Fairfax has written to her of preparations for Mr Rochester's wedding to Blanche. She arrives at sunset and meets Mr Rochester en route. She admits to him that 'wherever you are is my home — my only home.'

## Chapter XXIII

Jane meets Mr Rochester in the orchard on Midsummer's Eve. He goads her into a declaration of her feelings and an assertion of her independence. Under the chestnut tree, he asks her to marry him. When she can be persuaded of his sincerity, she agrees. Mr Rochester defies God and man. The weather changes suddenly, and lightning strikes the tree.

- 'Mrs Dionysius O'Gall of Bitternutt Lodge': Rochester is making up names to tease her, but she is too distressed to pick up on this.
- Charlotte Brontë defied nineteenth-century convention and outraged some critics by having Jane declare her passionate feelings for a man, especially one who is her social superior.
- 'I have her and will hold her': Rochester thinks of Jane as a possession.

## Chapter XXIV

The next day, Mr Rochester declares they will be married in four weeks. Jane feels both joy and fear at this announcement. She resists his attempts to shower her with jewels and make the world acknowledge her a beauty. Mrs Fairfax warns Jane to be on her guard. While shopping she feels degraded by his attempts to buy her extravagant gifts, as if he is treating her like a sultan would a slave. This makes her write to her uncle in the hopes of a small allowance. She keeps Mr Rochester at arm's length by teasing him during their courtship.

- 'wherever I stamped my hoof': Rochester implies that, when he travelled in Europe he was like a satyr, with the upper half of a man and the lower half of a goat. In classical mythology, satyrs were highly-sexed lovers of wine and women, ready for every physical pleasure. He sees her as a 'sylph', a spirit of the air, who will cleanse him of his sins.
- Charlotte Brontë wrote the song Mr Rochester sings, inspired by her love for Monsieur Heger.
- After the song, Brontë uses the third person pronoun 'he', even though their conversation is reported in quotation marks. This has the effect of distancing us from the conversation, which is intended to be an example of the way in which Jane kept him at a distance.
- The final words of the chapter reveal that Jane has not completed her journey to maturity. She needs to learn to put human love in its proper place and not to lose sight of God in her worship of Mr Rochester.

## Chapter XXV

The evening before the wedding, Mr Rochester is absent on business. Jane is apprehensive and waits for him in the orchard. She tells him that the previous night she dreamt of carrying an unknown child through the ruins of Thornfield. When she woke, a woman like the vampire was in her room. She lost consciousness, but next morning her veil was torn. Rochester reassures her that the woman was Grace Poole and tells her to sleep with Adèle.

- Instead of telling the story chronologically, Charlotte Brontë makes Jane withhold the knowledge of Bertha's visit until she tells Mr Rochester, thus increasing tension and suspense.
- In yet another reference to the moon, Brontë personifies it and describes it as bewildered and blood-red, as if it is trying to warn Jane.

- The chestnut tree continues to symbolise Jane and Mr Rochester's relationship. The word 'cloven' is the past participle of 'to cleave', which has opposite meanings of to split apart and to cling together.
- As in Chapter XXI, the dream of a child portends disaster, but the dream is also a premonition.
- Goethe's *The Bride of Corinth*, a Gothic horror story that features a female vampire, was published in translation in 1844 in *Blackwood's Magazine*, to which Reverend Brontë subscribed.

## Chapter XXVI

The morning of the wedding, a grim-faced Mr Rochester hurries Jane to the church. A stranger, a solicitor, declares the existence of a previous marriage, and Mr Mason, who has seen Jane's letter to her uncle, overcomes his fear to testify that his sister still lives. Mr Rochester takes them all to view his wife, who is imprisoned in the attic of Thornfield Hall and guarded by Grace Poole. Jane retreats to her room in despair and prays.

- 'Creole' is a term used for someone of European origin who was born in the West Indies, but it can also refer to someone of mixed race. This ambiguity fostered nineteenth-century prejudices against different races. In the next chapter, Mr Rochester tells Jane that he 'longed for what suited me — for the antipodes of the Creole'. The assumption is that Bertha is full of vices because she is a Creole.

## Chapter XXVII

Some hours later, Jane emerges from her room having decided that she must leave Thornfield. To persuade her that she would be morally right to stay, Mr Rochester tells her about his arranged marriage and the consequences. She says farewell and asks God to look after him. That night she slips away and takes a coach to an unknown, distant place.

- 'You shall yourself pluck out your right eye: yourself cut off your right hand': there are many references to the Bible throughout this novel. This one comes from the Sermon on the Mount where Christ is condemning sexual misconduct. Jane judges that it is her heart that has offended and must be punished. This reference foreshadows Mr Rochester's symbolic 'punishment' to his eye and his hand.
- 'I could not rid myself of it by any legal proceedings.' Until 1857, divorce could be obtained only by Act of Parliament, and, if one partner was mentally ill, it was impossible to obtain a legal separation.
- 'The Grimsby Retreat' refers to an asylum run by Quakers where mentally ill people were cared for humanely. Grace Poole does not care for Bertha according to Quaker values.

## Chapter XXVIII

Two days later, the coach leaves Jane on the moors. She is comforted by nature, prays and sleeps well. Next morning, having spent all her money on the coach fare, she is faint through lack of food. She walks to a nearby village, first asking for work and then begging for food. People are suspicious of a well-dressed beggar and shut her out. Eventually, she wanders to an isolated house on the moors and watches two kind-looking young ladies through the window. Jane knocks, a servant refuses to admit her, she collapses and is rescued by St John Rivers.

- Jane is set down at a crossroads, symbolic of choices she has to make.
- Praying for Mr Rochester, Jane 'felt the might and strength of God' and 'convinced I grew that neither earth should perish, nor one of the souls it treasured'. This is a turning point for Jane as she becomes convinced by Helen's doctrine that 'God will never destroy what he created', and that even sinners like Mr Rochester can be saved.
- 'I wished but this — that my Maker had that night thought good to require my soul of me whilst I slept.' Like Helen, Jane is tempted to embrace death to avoid 'further conflict', but suicide was considered a sin and a crime and she struggles on, determined to take responsibility for herself.
- Jane swoons as Mercy swooned outside the Wicket gate after struggling across the Slough of Despond, and she was lifted up by St John just as Mercy was lifted up by the keeper of the gate in *The Pilgrim's Progress*.

## Chapter XXIX

For three days, Jane lies ill. Then, when she recovers, she helps Hannah in the kitchen and learns more about her hosts. Old Mr Rivers, who has just died, lost his fortune through an unwise investment. His children have come home briefly to sort out his affairs, then Diana and Mary must return to their positions as governess. St John is the local clergyman. Jane tells the family some of her story and admits that she has not told them her real name. St John agrees to find her work.

- The man old Mr Rivers trusted was his brother-in-law, John Eyre.
- The closeness of the Rivers family reflects the closeness of Charlotte Brontë and her siblings.

## Chapter XXX

Jane lives happily with Diana and Mary, and she gratefully accepts St John's offer of a position as schoolmistress. The Rivers learn of the death of their wealthy but estranged uncle, but are disappointed in their hope that he planned to repair the wrong done to their father and leave them some of his fortune.

- Like the Brontës' Aunt Branwell, and Mr Brocklehurst, St John is a Calvinist, believing in predestination, i.e. that some souls have already been elected for salvation and the rest are destined for damnation, or 'reprobation'.

## Chapter XXXI

On her first evening in her new cottage, Jane struggles to overcome feelings that she is degraded by her occupation. St John comes to the door and delivers a lecture about the necessity to 'turn the bent of nature' and explains why he wants to be a missionary. Rosamond Oliver arrives and it is obvious that he is struggling to repress his love for her.

- The 'riots' of which Rosamond speaks might be references to the Luddites, who destroyed machinery in protest against losing their jobs through the mechanisation of the textile industry, or they may refer to civil rights demonstrations such as that in St Peter's Field, Manchester, which were violently dispersed by the militia.

## Chapter XXXII

Jane settles comfortably into her new home, but every night her passionate feelings for Mr Rochester are released in her dreams. On waking, she represses these longings and appears tranquil by the time school starts. Rosamond Oliver visits her, often when St John is teaching, and is impressed by Jane's sketches, asking Jane to sketch her portrait. Mr Oliver visits and invites Jane to Vale Hall. When St John sees the portrait, he tears a strip from the paper Jane uses as a hand-rest and he departs mysteriously.

## Chapter XXXIII

St John returns next day in a snow storm, his suspicions that she is the missing heiress confirmed by her name idly written on the edge of the paper. Delighted, she determines to share her fortune with her new-found cousins.

- Charlotte Brontë spins out the mystery by having St John tell the story slowly and teasingly rather than confronting Jane at once. This way the knowledge dawns on us slowly, so that we can empathise with Jane's pleasure at finding a family.
- 'I carried my point': Jane is still legally a minor, so she needs two judges to approve her decision.

## Chapter XXXIV

Jane moves back to Moor House just before Christmas. She and Hannah spring-clean the house and Jane refurbishes it tastefully. St John disapproves of what he sees as a waste of her talents. As the girls settle down, Jane teaches herself to read German, but St John asks her to help him learn Hindustani. In her dealings with the solicitor she asks about Mr Rochester, and then writes twice to Mrs Fairfax, who does not reply. In May, St John asks her to accompany him to India as his wife. She is tempted by the idea of missionary work, but agrees to go only as his companion. St John is deeply offended by her.

- 'since those days I have seen paysannes and Bäuerinnen': this is the only reference to Mr Rochester and Jane's travels in Europe.
- 'Looked to river, looked to hill': this is the last of several references to Sir Walter Scott's *The Lay of the Last Minstrel*, in which the hero and heroine, after many troubles, eventually marry for love.

## Chapter XXXV

St John rejects Jane's overtures of friendship and she repeats her refusal to marry him, claiming: 'If I were to marry you, you would kill me. You are killing me now.' He is shocked at her 'unfeminine' behaviour. A week later, she admits to being 'thrilled' by his evening prayers and almost yields to his will. She entreats heaven to show her the path, and, as if miraculously, hears Mr Rochester's voice calling her name. She goes to her room and prays.

- 'God did not give me my life to throw away': in this her beliefs differ from Helen's. She has found her own interpretation of religion.
- 'castaway': like Mr Brocklehurst in Chapter VII, St John fears she is already damned.
- 'to have yielded now would have been an error of judgment': Jane has been tested again and resisted a different kind of temptation.
- Charlotte Brontë once told her friend, Mary Taylor, that phantom voices dictated her poetry.

## Chapter XXXVI

Jane returns to Thornfield and finds it burnt to a shell. The landlord of The Rochester Arms tells her that Bertha set fire to the house and then threw herself off the battlements, and that Mr Rochester was maimed and blinded trying to rescue her.

- 'To prolong doubt was to prolong hope': Brontë keeps the reader in suspense as Jane walks to Thornfield and tells us her thoughts.
- 'Hear an illustration, reader.' Jane is a self-conscious narrator, deliberately shaping her narrative to prolong the suspense.
- Another method of drawing out the tension is to have the story eventually told in a long-winded and confusing way by old Mr Rochester's butler.
- Mr Rochester's attempt to save Bertha is his first step towards his redemption.
- The fire is both a symbolic warning of the destructiveness of unrestrained passion, and also a means of purifying Mr Rochester by punishing and redeeming him.

## Chapter XXXVII

Jane goes straight to Ferndean, reveals herself to Mr Rochester, teases him out of his depression and encourages him to propose to her. She accepts, and he tells her of his prayer to God before crying out her name. The coincidence that he did this at just the same time as she heard his voice fills her with awe, but she does not tell him. He thanks God and entreats him to help him lead a purer life.

- Unlike in Chapter XXIII when Mr Rochester manipulated Jane into declaring her love for him, this time Jane controls the conversation, makes Mr Rochester jealous and forces him to declare his feelings first.
- 'Apollo', the sun god of classical mythology, represents the ideal male physique. 'Vulcan' was the ancient Roman god of destructive, devouring fire, who became patron of blacksmiths.

## Chapter XXXVIII (Conclusion)

Ten years later, Jane brings her supposed autobiography to a close, telling her readers that she and Mr Rochester married, are blissfully happy and have children. She arranged for Adèle to go to a more indulgent school and she has become a pleasing young lady. Diana and Mary are both happily married and Jane and Mr Rochester meet them once a year. Jane corresponds regularly with St John, who is dying but joyful at the thought of his reward in heaven.

- 'Reader, I married him.' It is interesting that Jane thinks of herself as the prime mover in this marriage, rather than saying: 'We were married.'
- While she was writing *Jane Eyre*, Brontë was caring for her father, who was having an operation to remove cataracts.

# Characters

## Jane

Jane is a poor orphan whose mother was disowned by her parents when she married someone of whom they disapproved, and whose father was a poor clergyman. The novel follows her development from a ten-year-old child, dependent on the charity of her aunt who resents her, to a mature woman who has achieved self-knowledge, independence and a marriage with her intellectual equal.

As a child she is passionate, but nervous and highly strung. She has a strongly developed sense of justice and of her own worth, in spite of the Reed family's attempts to humble her. She also has a strong need to love and be loved, and she lavishes her thwarted love on a doll. Having learned that vengeance leaves a sour aftertaste, Jane learns to control her temper at Lowood and to mask her feelings behind an apparent calmness.

We follow her life as her self-discipline and integrity are put to the test, as she learns to balance feeling and judgement, as she achieves independence and equality with the man she loves, and as she finds her own understanding of religion out of the different doctrines presented to her.

Charlotte Brontë uses Jane to voice the author's judgement on other characters. This means that Jane can appear cold and unfeeling when she writes about children, intellectually snobbish when she writes about Mrs Fairfax, Rosamond Oliver and the children at her school, too quickly judgemental when she describes Mr Mason, and, to a modern reader, full of racial prejudices when she writes about Adèle with her 'French defects', the 'ignorant' Indians and the 'enslaved' in Eastern cultures.

## Mr Rochester

Mr Rochester is dark and brooding rather than good looking, and he is muscular and stocky, rather than tall and elegant, like a conventional romantic hero. He is arrogant and domineering, brusque and quick-tempered, passionate and energetic. At their second meeting, he tells Jane that he was not always embittered and hard, and it soon becomes apparent that he is haunted by something that happened in his youth and regrets the sinful and dissipated way he has lived. He seeks reformation and has decided that the way to redeem himself is through Jane's innocence.

In almost every respect, Mr Rochester is a Byronic hero. However, he lacks political passion, being totally self-centred, and neither dies as freedom fighter nor a monk, although he does turn to God at the end of the novel. By the end he has learned to take responsibility for his own actions and to live within the confines of God's laws, but he is still jealous and possessive, preventing Jane from continuing as Adèle's governess. Jane is not only sexually attracted to him, she also loves him because she does not need to put on an act with him and can be completely herself. He is her intellectual equal and he values her highly. She feels she understands him and it makes her feel good that she knows how to deal with him and tease him out of his moods. Mr Rochester appeals to that side of Jane's nature that yearns to love and to be loved for itself.

## St John Rivers

St John appeals to the side of Jane's nature that aspires to something great and that wants to sacrifice itself to the service of God. She admires St John for his intellect, his religious faith and his zeal. However, she thinks he is wrong to deny his nature and embrace martyrdom and, though she is tempted by the path he offers her, she refuses to abandon that side of her nature which needs human love and self-fulfilment.

A year before he meets Jane, St John thought he had made a mistake entering the ministry. He was ambitious for worldly renown and yearned for earthly glory. Once he realised that, as a missionary, he could gain an incorruptible crown in heaven, he determined to subjugate everything to this one ambition. He suppresses his burning love for Rosamond, ignores the love and needs of his sisters, leaves to another his work among the poor in the parish of Morton, and he observes Jane closely, testing her character, with a view to marrying her to assist him in his ministry. He is hurt by the scorn she pours on his proposal the first time he asks her. The second time he is visibly pained, and yet he perseveres and gently tries a third time to persuade her. Perhaps Jane is misjudging him — perhaps he feels for her more than he admits.

Through considering St John's proposal, Jane realises that, with St John as her husband, she would never be able to act naturally, so, paradoxically, her freedom and independence are to be found in a relationship of mutual emotional dependence, where husband and wife come together as equals.

## Helen Burns

Like St John, Helen has sublimated her passion into religious ecstasy but, whereas St John is ambitious for glory, Helen's religion is one of self-denial. She seems too good to be true: she epitomises Christ's teaching of loving your neighbours and turning the other cheek, as she endures Miss Scatcherd's bullying without complaint, even admitting culpability. However, this can be read as a form of passive resistance that actually goads her persecutor to be more cruel and puts herself in the role of martyr.

When Jane first meets her, Helen is reading Samuel Johnson's *Rasselas*, a book that argues that surrender and self-control will enable us to bear with the difficulties of life. Helen is dying of tuberculosis and she embraces the idea of death as a release from the harshness and injustice of life on earth. She offers a contrasting form of belief to the harsh creed of Mr Brocklehurst, being convinced that salvation is open to all. She is an inspirational character whose influence remains with Jane throughout her life.

## Bertha

Bertha is never developed as a character. We learn her history through the biased narrative of Mr Rochester, and we see her only after she has been 'embruted' by ten years of solitary confinement in a room with no windows and no mental stimulation.

Bertha's presence is not essential to the plot, only the fact that Mr Rochester is already married, so her role in the novel is largely symbolic. She has been variously interpreted as representative of the British Empire's attitude to other cultures, as symbolic of the Victorian wife, trapped in the home, or as a manifestation of Jane's subconscious feelings of rage against injustice and fear of her sexual desires, which she has learned to suppress. Bertha certainly acts as a warning of the consequences of a woman allowing passion to rule her behaviour.

Her most important function is to be the Gothic horror element and to raise the suspense and tension through her preternatural laugh, her blood-sucking vampiric behaviour and her goblin appearance.

## Miss Temple

Miss Temple is an elegant, beautiful, cultured woman, compassionate and fair-minded. She listens to Jane's version of the events at Gateshead, verifies it, and clears her name before the whole school. Jane's feelings for Miss Temple verge on hero worship, and it is from Miss Temple that Jane gains her passion for self-improvement. She also learns self-control from Miss Temple, who, Charlotte Brontë suggests, has an equally passionate sense of injustice and hatred of hypocrisy. She knows, however, when resistance could be worse than useless and her face turns to marble as Mr Brocklehurst rebukes her for her kindness to the girls. While Miss Temple is at Lowood, Jane regards it as home but, once she is married, Jane is restless and the school becomes like a prison from which she desires liberty.

## Mr Brocklehurst

Mr Brocklehurst is presented through the eyes of a ten-year-old child, and so he appears a caricature of a pompous, self-righteous hypocrite. He is described as a black pillar, cold, hard and unbending, with features like those of the cruel wolf in *Little Red Riding Hood*. We are invited to laugh at his insistence that the girls should be shorn of curls and wear plain, unflattering clothes, while his own family are over-dressed and wear artificial curls. There is something sinister about the way he inspects the girls' underwear on the washing line and tries to suppress their emerging womanhood with poor and inadequate food and ill-fitting childish uniforms.

Mr Brocklehurst's behaviour reveals that this supposedly charitable institution is not there for the benefit of the girls, but to perpetuate the injustice in society and fit them for the humble roles assigned to them. He acts as a contrast both to Helen Burns, whose faith totally contradicts his, and to St John Rivers, who preaches the same doctrine, but who lives by what he preaches.

## The Reed family

Because the Reeds are shown filtered through Jane's resentment, they are totally unsympathetic characters, although Jane does begin to pity Mrs Reed as she lies dying. Mrs Reed was jealous of her husband's love for his sister, Jane's mother, and so she resents having to look after her orphaned niece. Mrs Reed also feels guilty because she is not bringing Jane up as if she were her own child, as her husband had made her promise on his deathbed. Jane's outburst spells this out to her and, when Mrs Reed lies to her brother-in-law, John Eyre, it is done out of revenge for Jane's childish attack. Her breaking of her promise to her husband on his deathbed and her lie to his brother torment her final hours, so she is unable to accept Jane's offer of reconciliation.

Jane's cousins take their lead from their mother, and they not only exclude her, but John actually bullies her. None of them emerge as rounded characters. At a significant time in Jane's development, just before Mr Rochester proposes to her, we are invited to compare her with Eliza, who represents judgement without feeling, and with Georgiana, who represents feeling without judgement. John is a total contrast to his namesake, St John Rivers, and is a good Victorian example of what happens to a boy when he is indulged as a child.

## Diana and Mary

Jane's other cousins are women whom Jane admires and with whom she feels in perfect sympathy. They represent that harmonious balance between judgement and feeling that Jane needs to achieve.

## Blanche

Mr Rochester compares Blanche with Bertha before he married her, and, if Bertha was indeed like Blanche, beautiful, arrogant, cruel to her social inferiors and self-willed, it is easy to see why Mr Rochester confined her to the attic. If he had married Blanche, there would doubtless have been a short battle of wills before Mr Rochester conquered and broke her, with no feelings of guilt. He feels no qualms about using her to make Jane jealous, saying: 'Her feelings are concentrated in one — pride; and that needs humbling.'

## Mrs Fairfax

When her clergyman husband died, Mrs Fairfax accepted a position as housekeeper to a distant relative, Edward Fairfax Rochester. She is kind and warm-hearted and, to some extent, she acts as a substitute mother to Jane, warning her to be on her guard when Mr Rochester asks to marry her. Brontë uses her as a plot device to provide Jane, and the reader, with limited information about Thornfield, its owner, and his guests.

## Rosamond Oliver

Jane is intellectually snobbish towards Rosamond, declaring her 'not profoundly interesting or thoroughly impressive', so readers must judge for themselves whether in this Jane is a reliable narrator. Rosamond is not merely beautiful and charming, she is a true philanthropist. She has persuaded her father to finance schools for the children of the poor and, out of her own allowance, she has furnished the schoolmistress's cottage and paid for the education and clothing of a servant.

Unlike the other rich characters in the novel, Rosamond is not at all snobbish, treating Jane as a friend and encouraging St John to propose to her, even though he is just a poor clergyman. She flirts with him, but is sensitive and thoughtful, rebuking herself when she remembers that St John will be sad because his sisters have had to return to their positions as governesses. She does not really love St John, however, and, when he makes clear his intention to go to India as a missionary without her, she marries the grandson and heir to Sir Frederick Granby. Since her own grandfather was a journeyman needlemaker, Brontë is using her to represent the rapid rise of the families of working-class entrepreneurs in the Industrial Revolution.

## Servants

Brontë has a keen ear for the dialogue of servants, and this helps her to depict them economically but realistically. They have an important function in keeping the sometimes extraordinary events of the novel rooted in the ordinary world. Mary and John, at Ferndean, talk in a broad Yorkshire dialect, are stolid and loyal, pragmatic and 'phlegmatic'. Hannah also speaks broad Yorkshire, but she loves to talk and is fiercely protective of the Rivers family.

Brontë uses no dialect features for the servants at Gateshead, presumably to differentiate house servants from servants lower in the hierarchy. Miss Abbott, the lady's maid, reflects her mistress's prejudices and preferences, but Bessie does try to stand up for Jane. She is the one person Jane clings to when she leaves Gateshead. Bessie is a warm, good-hearted girl, although quick to scold and, before she leaves, Jane learns to appreciate her essential kindness and not to be afraid of her.

Bessie's ballads and folklore stay with Jane throughout the novel, and they are a significant influence on her imagination. Bessie visits Jane at Lowood and tells her about her uncle's visit, thus preparing us for the time when her aunt summons her. When she revisits Gateshead, Bessie's warm welcome provides a sharp contrast to the coldness of the Reed family.

# Autobiography: Chapter I

Having selected fictional autobiography as her narrative technique for *Jane Eyre*, Brontë considered her choices as a novelist very carefully. She starts Jane's autobiography with the incident that marks the first time she has resisted John's bullying and fought back. This is also the first time Jane tries to analyse her feelings and put her story into words for someone else, Mr Lloyd, the apothecary. This leads to the next stage in her life, at Lowood Institution. Until this point, Jane has been unhappy, but there has been no dramatic focus to interest readers.

As the novel opens, the weather is cold and forbidding, and Brontë juxtaposes the outside scene with a warm family scene at the fireside. We realise that Jane, however, is excluded from this scene because the family are also cold and forbidding. They humble her with a consciousness of her physical inferiority, and are keeping her at a distance until she acquires 'a more sociable and child-like disposition'. We could say that the weather takes on a symbolic meaning, representing the coldness and loneliness of Jane's world. The view from the window seat reflects Jane's own misery, and it is obscured by mist. This suggests that she cannot see beyond her own unhappiness, that her future was also obscured by 'a pale blank of mist and cloud'. However, just as the mist outside will lift, so her future will emerge more clearly, and Brontë has opened the story at the point when her life is about to change.

Jane is presented as an outsider, resented by the family as a poor relation foisted on them by Mr Reed, who seems to remain the head of the household even after his death. Jane is also resented by the servants as 'less than a servant, for you do nothing for your keep'. Reminders of her ambiguous position within the household have made her deeply unhappy and unable to behave in the same manner as her cousins, who are lovingly indulged. Not only is she excluded from the family circle, but she is also persecuted by John, who seeks her out to bully her.

Jane finds refuge in the inner world of her imagination. Brontë reveals this in the way she responds to the pictures in Bewick's *History of British Birds*. In one picture, for instance, she sees two becalmed ships as 'phantoms', and she passes quickly over 'the fiend pinning down the thief's pack behind him' and 'the black, horned thing seated aloof on a rock, surveying a distant crowd surrounding a gallows'. These are objects of terror for her, but each tells her a mysterious story and feeds the imagination that produced the paintings she later showed to Mr Rochester. These pictures give a sense of foreboding and foreshadow the events to come, introducing elements of the Gothic genre. Brontë draws on this isolation, the association with death (the wreck, the churchyard and the gallows) and the workings of the supernatural (the ghastly moon, the phantoms and the fiend), as well as the presence of some undefined evil, in other contexts throughout the novel.

From her greater maturity, the adult Jane is able to guide the reader to be aware of the limited perceptions of the child. As little Jane looks at the pictures of birds in 'forlorn regions of dreary space', she tells us that from them she formed an idea of her own. The pictures acted as a stimulus for her own imagination, but she helps us appreciate that this was 'shadowy, like all the half-comprehended notions that float dim through children's brains, but strangely impressive'. Brontë clearly wants to establish them as formative influences on Jane's as yet 'undeveloped understanding and imperfect feelings'.

The first chapter is successful as an introduction to Jane's supposed autobiography because we are introduced to Jane as she is about to leave Gateshead and embark on her growth to maturity and her struggle to attain self-fulfilment. We are introduced to key aspects of her personality, such as her passionate nature and her vivid imagination, as well as her awareness of her plain appearance and preference for avoiding society. We are also made aware of her deeply felt sense of justice and refusal to submit to bullying.

Brontë has introduced symbols that she will develop throughout the novel. The weather outside, and the book she looks at, seem to represent Jane's inner world. The scarlet curtains, which envelop the window seat, suggest a comfortable womb-like space where she can feel safe. Brontë introduces the juxtaposition of fire and ice, heat and cold, passion and coldness. Jane's ambiguous social standing sets up most of the novel's internal tension and conflict, and her struggle against male oppression begins with John Reed.

As she writes about her childhood, we learn something of how Jane has matured into an adult. She continues to be an avid reader. As a child she was familiar with Bewick's book as well as Goldsmith's *History of Rome*, but she also quotes from a poem by James Thompson and makes references to novels by Samuel Richardson and Henry Brooke. Knowing that Jane is a passionate character with a vivid imagination, Brontë may be warning us that Jane might not be an entirely reliable narrator. Her memories may be highly coloured, and her desire to present her story as a Cinderella-style fairy tale may lead her to exaggerate.

*Marx*

# The red-room: Chapter II

Jane finds her position in the household confusing. She is a member of the family and therefore not expected to associate with the servants, but she is a poor relation and therefore totally dependent on the Reeds' charity. If she displeases Mrs Reed, she is at risk of being sent to the poor-house, so it is her 'place to be humble, and to try to make [herself] agreeable to them'. It is not surprising that the mature Jane tells us 'this reproach of my dependence had become a vague sing-song in my ear; very painful and crushing, but only half intelligible'. She is told that John Reed is her 'young master', and yet she is not a servant — she belongs in the same class as her cousins. The only difference is that whereas 'they will have a great deal of money...you will have none'. (The irony is that John will dissipate their fortune, whereas Jane will inherit her uncle's wealth.) Mrs Reed will release her from her prison only 'on condition of perfect submission and stillness'.

The threat to bind Jane to a chair is one of a number of hints Brontë gives us that there is some comparison or parallel to be drawn between Jane and Bertha. While Jane is behaving 'like a mad cat', locking her up in solitary confinement does not teach her to behave in the manner expected of her, but induces a temporary madness in the form of a fit. This invites us to question how much of Bertha's present madness can be attributed to her solitary incarceration.

Miss Abbott looks 'darkly and doubtfully' on Jane, who interprets her look to mean that she doubted her sanity, but it seems to be more than that. Miss Abbott calls her 'an underhand little thing', as if she fears that Jane might upset the accepted hierarchy of the house. Her quiet, reserved manner did indeed conceal just the kind of resentment and anger at injustice that becomes open rebellion.

Brontë has already established that 'the folds of scarlet drapery' round the window seat give Jane a sense of warmth and security, with a hint of a 'back to the womb' image. This hiding-place works symbolically to represent withdrawal into the world of her imagination. The red-room is also a hushed, shadowy, enclosed space, but here she is locked in, prey to the darker side of her imagination and her superstitious fear of Mr Reed's ghost. When the inner world of her imagination is not an escape but a prison, it can quickly turn into a nightmarish experience.

Like all the other houses in this book, except Ferndean, this is a house apparently run by women, but, in reality, it is ruled by a man. Mr Reed still dominates the household from the grave. Mrs Reed keeps Jane only because of 'a hard-wrung pledge' to her husband on his deathbed. The room in which he died is kept virtually untouched, like a shrine to his memory. The bed in which he died is 'like a tabernacle', housing a divine covenant. The chair near the head of the bed is 'like a pale throne', empty, but still symbolic of the ruler of this household. In a secret drawer is a miniature painting of Mr Reed. So, even after nine years, he still rules the house and, symbolically, even Jane's inner consciousness. There is, of course, one male member of the family ready to inherit his father's place: 'John no one thwarted, much less punished', even though he is tyrannical, cruel, destructive and rude to his mother. The reason for Jane's imprisonment is her rebellion against his assumption of power over her. The women in the house uphold this system of patriarchy, supporting the concept of male dominance and power.

Apart from the 'snowy' white bed and chair that enhance the religious imagery, the room is, as its name states, red. It is fitted out with 'red carpet', 'deep red damask' curtains round the bed and at the windows, and a crimson cloth over the table. It is a colour more associated with a room in the 'red-light district' than a death-chamber, and such excess of redness suggests passion and, indeed, sexuality. Jane is ten, approaching puberty, so perhaps Brontë intends this episode to be seen as a kind of rite of passage, an initiation into the mystery of female sexuality, a time when she must put childhood behind her and come to terms with being a woman. At the beginning of the next chapter, Jane wakes to 'a terrible red glare, crossed with thick black bars'; it took her five minutes to recognise this as the nursery fire. This is a powerful image of how the safety of childhood has turned into a vivid image of confined passion.

This interpretation is supported by her confusion as she looks in the mirror. Jane does not recognise herself in 'the strange little figure there gazing at me'. This figure she describes as 'half fairy, half imp'. The night before the broken wedding, she sees another strange figure in her mirror, and once again she 'became insensible from terror'. In *The Madwoman in the Attic*, Gilbert and Gubar say 'a mirror, after all, is also a sort of chamber, a mysterious enclosure in which images of the self are trapped like "divers parchments"'. Perhaps we could interpret this image as Brontë's way of showing Jane's fear of her sexuality and her passionate nature at two key moments in her life.

It is worth analysing the ways in which Brontë builds up the child's growing sense of terror. At first the child looks around the room. The bed linen 'glared' comfortlessly white, and the atmosphere was 'chill', 'silent', 'remote', 'lonely', even the dust was 'quiet'. The list of the contents of the secret drawer builds up to the portrait of the deceased husband, which Jane describes as the 'spell'. Under this spell, Jane sees the bed as a 'tabernacle', the curtains as 'shrouds' and the chair as a 'throne', evoking thoughts of death and judgement. Even her own reflection in the mirror is transformed into a 'strange' but fascinating figure with 'glittering' eyes, which reminds her of 'the tiny phantoms, half fairy, half imp' that featured in Bessie's stories.

Superstition was taking hold of Jane's imagination, 'but it was not yet her hour for complete victory'. This personification shows how the child was at the mercy of things beyond her control. The tension is eased somewhat as Jane remembers her grievances and, in another personification, 'Resolve' instigated thoughts of running away or starving herself to death. The tension gradually builds again as she listens to the beating rain and the howling wind and realises that, if she succeeds, she will be put in the vault under the church with Mr Reed. This reminds her that, according to superstition, spirits are supposed to revisit 'the earth to punish the perjured and avenge the oppressed'.

Brontë has shown how Jane's mind has been prepared for horror and her nerves shaken by agitation, so, fearing that Mr Reed's ghost was coming to comfort her, she interprets a strange moving light as 'a herald of some coming vision from another world'. Her growing terror is conveyed in the short, abrupt, monosyllabic clauses: 'My heart beat thick, my head grew hot; a sound filled my ears' — her absolute panic in the breathless syntax of 'something seemed near me; I was oppressed, suffocated: endurance broke down'.

As a mature woman, Jane Rochester still feels the pain of rejection and the anger at the injustice, but she has learned to temper this with understanding, although the words she chooses suggest that she has not forgiven. Four times she refers to the young Jane as a 'thing' when she is explaining why she was an outsider at Gateshead Hall. This non-human epithet suggests that, at the time of writing, she is still indignant that they could not treat her like a human being, with feelings and emotional needs. However, with hindsight, she now understands that her aunt saw her as 'a precocious actress...she sincerely looked on [Jane] as a compound of virulent passions, mean spirit and dangerous duplicity'.

Later, when Jane tells Miss Temple what happened, she explains to her readers that 'I never forgot the, to me, frightful episode of the red-room...nothing could soften in my recollection the spasm of agony which clutched my heart when Mrs Reed spurned my wild application for pardon, and locked me a second time in the dark and haunted chamber' (Chapter VIII). It is significant that she remembers Mrs Reed's rejection as a physical pain, and there is a strong suggestion that the adult still feels that pain. Another time, after deciding that she must leave Mr Rochester, she 'dreamt [she] lay in the red-room at Gateshead; that the night was dark, and [her] mind impressed with strange fears', only this time the strange light is the moon. The red-room appears as a memory whenever Jane makes a connection between her current situation and that time of humiliation, exclusion and imprisonment. It becomes symbolic of what Jane must overcome in her struggle to find freedom, self-respect and a sense of belonging. She must overcome the male assumption of superiority embodied first in John Reed, then Mr Brocklehurst, and then Mr Rochester. She must come to terms with her own passions and sexuality, find a balance between reason and feeling.

# Narrative technique: Chapter XIX

Brontë's choice of a pseudo-autobiography for the form of her novel gives it an essential unity in spite of the different settings. The structure of the novel is organised around Jane's quest for her own identity, with each of its five parts representing a different stage in her development. However, a first-person narrative, written with hindsight, can be flat and dull if the writer does not employ techniques to create the appearance of spontaneity and to preserve the mystery. Brontë wants her readers to experience events as Jane did, with her limited knowledge and understanding.

To this end she withholds the information that her narrator is actually Jane Rochester until the final chapter, and the mature Jane tells her story with only occasional observations on events. Jane is aware of her readers, sometimes addressing them directly, but she gives no hint of the final outcome. At some key points she employs the present tense to give events a dramatic immediacy, but Brontë usually uses the past tense to suggest that Jane is remembering what happened.

In Chapter XIX, Brontë preserves the mystery for her readers by letting us view the scene as it was played out, without Jane Rochester's subsequent knowledge. This way she can keep the gypsy's identity secret until Jane Eyre realises who the 'woman' really is. Brontë's narrative technique brings the scene alive, as if it is being played out in front of us rather than narrated from a distance of some 11 years. Most of this chapter is dialogue, with little input by the narrator except to act as stage directions. At the beginning of Chapter XI Brontë compares a new chapter in a novel with a new scene in a play, and this scene reads very like a play. Every little detail of the conversation is recorded, even when Mr Rochester pauses to find the best way of putting into words what he believes to be Jane's feelings for him, and she interrupts with 'I what?'

The fire is at the centre of this stage set. Mr Rochester has extinguished the candle to aid his disguise, and he is bending over the fire, which provides the only light in the room. He positions himself carefully so that his face is in shadow but Jane's is illuminated, as he makes her kneel and look up to him while he examines her face. The second time Mr Rochester tells Jane to kneel by the fire, she complains that 'the fire scorches me'. Brontë uses the image of flames to represent sexual desire and symbolically Jane retreats from it as something dangerous. Previously, when Brontë used this fire imagery (perhaps more explicitly), and Rochester's bed was on fire, it was Jane who doused the flames. Mr Rochester observes that 'no contact strikes the fire from you that is in you', and he notices that 'the flame flickers in the eye'. He can recognise the passion within Jane, but he does not know how to release it.

After the charades, in which Mr Rochester assumes a number of different identities, he assumes yet another role. Appearances can be deceptive, and we are invited to wonder whether the Mr Rochester Jane thinks she knows is yet another disguise. The narrator preserves the visitor's anonymity by using various epithets to create an appropriately mysterious atmosphere. Even in the enlightened twenty-first century, 'gypsies' are still regarded with suspicion. Travelling people are outsiders, and society fears them as threats to the conventional way of life. They are often used in detective fiction as sinister figures, foreign in appearance if not in origin, although true gypsies are dark-skinned Romanies. When Mr Rochester dresses up as a gypsy, he knowingly takes on a persona that his guests will fear, not just for supposed psychic powers, but also because he threatens the harmony of the house, symbolised in the darkness of his appearance and the room. When Jane refers to him as 'the rigorous Sybil', she is referring to a female enchantress in Greek mythology. Half-human, half-nymph, the Sybil could read the past and foretell the future. He is also called a 'crone', which was originally an old useless ewe and was later used metaphorically as a word for a withered old woman, and a 'strange being', which sounds non-human.

Brontë juxtaposes Mr Rochester's decision to ask Jane to marry him with the appearance of Mr Mason. Hearing of Bertha's brother's arrival precisely as he decides to commit bigamy gives him a blow that makes him stagger. However, the reader sees only his dramatic reaction, and, like Jane, does not know the reason. Nevertheless, when she realises the 'gypsy's' true identity, four short questions convey her confusion. Her concern is that she may have revealed her inner feelings; ironically, it is to Mr Rochester, not the 'gypsy' that she admits 'I'd give my life to serve you.'

Jane lets her guard down when the 'gypsy' speaks of Mr Rochester's gratitude at Blanche Ingram's attentions, but Jane Rochester does not admit to allowing jealousy to cloud her judgement. She claims that the 'gypsy' wielded an almost magical power over her, and that she was 'involved in a web of mystification'. Once again she blames an external force for casting a sort of spell on her, rather than admit to her own weakness, in this case jealousy.

Mr Rochester wants an opportunity to study Jane's face closely so that he can decide what to do. He also seems to be trying to trap her into revealing her feelings for him. His study confirms his fear that she will not agree to be his mistress, so he decides to offer her marriage, even though he is not free. However, the scene is more than a mere plot device; it adds to the Gothic tone of the novel, as well as creating more mystery as to the reason for Mr Rochester's desperate fear of Mr Mason. It could be that Brontë has another motive in dressing her hero up as a woman. Possibly she is questioning the traditional male and female roles, exploring Mr Rochester's dependence on Jane, even when he thinks he is in control, and anticipating the future when he will be forced by his injuries to assume a more passive role and Jane a more active one.

An important technique Brontë uses to establish character is to employ two pseudo-sciences that were popular at the time. 'Physiognomy' is interpreting the signs of the face, and 'phrenology' is interpreting the signs of the skull, because various parts of the head were thought to be responsible for different personal qualities. Mr Rochester studies Jane's face to assess her character, saying that Destiny is written 'in the face: on the forehead, about the eyes, in the eyes themselves, in the lines of the mouth'.

Brontë makes use of physiognomy and phrenology at other points in the novel as well. On p. 56, Jane admits to 'a considerable organ of veneration' to explain her 'admiring awe' of Miss Temple. On p. 154, Mr Rochester points to the 'prominences' that were supposed to indicate a strong conscience. When Jane is rescued by St John Rivers, he reads her character in her face: 'Rather an unusual physiognomy; certainly, not indicative of vulgarity or degradation... I trace lines of force in her face which make me sceptical of her tractability.' In each case, the 'sciences' read the character accurately. It is interesting to note that Brontë herself went to a phrenologist under an assumed name to have her own skull read.

In a first-person narrative, it is difficult for a novelist to reveal the thoughts of other characters, so Brontë makes Mr Rochester talk to himself. Once he has achieved his purpose and confirmed that, for Jane 'judgment shall still have the last word in every argument, and the casting vote in every decision', Mr Rochester drops his assumed voice and speaks his thoughts aloud, regardless of the fact that Jane is listening. It reads more like a soliloquy, especially when he admits his weakness in the face of his desire for Jane: 'So far I have governed myself thoroughly. I have acted as I inwardly swore I would act; but farther might try me beyond strength.'

The unity of the novel is greatly enhanced by the use of foreshadowing to prepare us for something that will happen later. In this chapter, Mr Rochester concludes that Jane's resolve could be articulated as: 'Strong wind, earthquake-shock, and fire may pass by; but I [Jane] shall follow the guiding of that still, small voice which interprets the dictates of conscience.' Like the prophet Elijah in 1 Kings 19, Jane will stand firm if 'a great and strong wind' threatens her, 'and after the wind an earthquake...and after the earthquake a fire'; he knows she will listen to the 'still small voice of God'. He did not realise how true his prophecy was. When her world is turned upside down and her emotions are in turmoil, she follows her conscience and leaves Thornfield. Another example of foreshadowing is Mr Rochester's collapse on hearing of Mr Mason's arrival. For the second time he has to lean on Jane's shoulder, and we are reminded of this at Ferndean, where Jane supports him because he is crippled and blind.

# Reading between the lines: Chapter XXIII

Brontë introduces Chapter XXIII with a long description that sets the appropriate Romantic mood. The first three paragraphs offer a very visual description of a dramatic sunset painted in words, and Brontë successfully evokes Jane's mood as she revels in the beauty of the evening. The setting sun is described in words from the semantic field of royalty; it leaves the scene 'in simple *state* — pure of the *pomp* of clouds', leaving behind the royal colours of 'solemn purple, burning with the light of red jewel and furnace flame'. This drama in the west is contrasted with the 'charm' of the east, where a 'fine, deep blue' sky has but 'one modest gem, a rising and solitary star'. The star sparkles like a jewel but is likened to a young girl who is unassuming and does not seek to compete with her glorious counterpart. Soon, however, the east will 'boast' the moon, with whom Jane has a particular affinity. This detailed and metaphorical description gives valuable insights into Jane's feelings as she enters the garden. Nineteenth-century conventions prevented Brontë from allowing Jane to admit her feelings, but the pathetic fallacy is a valuable device for revealing them and heightening the dramatic tension before this crucial scene. This is typical of the way Romantic writers use nature to suggest deeply passionate feelings when it is not appropriate or acceptable to state them in the manner we have come to expect in the modern world. Jane's appreciation of the sunset's power and beauty suggests that she feels passionately and has a heart that responds to such Romantic moments.

As Jane enters the orchard, Brontë uses dramatic irony to evoke anticipation in the reader. Jane smells the 'well-known scent' of a cigar, and she realises that Mr Rochester is standing at the slightly open library window and that she could be seen. She turns aside into the orchard before Mr Rochester sees her, but the reader anticipates his following her. Through Jane's description of the orchard, Brontë is able to suggest Jane's mood as she wanders there.

Jane describes the garden as 'Eden-like', a metaphor that suggests to the reader not only an innocent paradise but also the place where Eve was tempted. The orchard is separated from the house and garden by a high wall and a row of beeches, but only by a sunken fence from 'lonely fields'. This suggests closeness to nature and a distance from civilisation, i.e. this is a place where one can respond naturally to one's feelings without worrying about social conventions. The fragrance of the flowers is described as 'incense', suggesting a heady drug. Jane notices the early ripening cherries and gooseberries large as plums. This imagery carries a suggestion of fertility and has connotations of the fruit of the Garden of Eden. The moth, which Mr Rochester describes as 'so large and gay a night-rover', is unusually 'great' and helps to give an exotic feel to the garden, supported by Mr Rochester's comparison of it with insects in the West Indies. Another, essential, ingredient of a Romantic setting is 'the now-rising moon'.

Jane's description of the smell of the cigar as a 'fragrance', a 'scent' and a 'perfume' suggests that she finds it seductive rather than repellent. This could only be because of its association with Mr Rochester, so the reader realises that she loves him before she admits it, even to herself. When Jane realises that Mr Rochester is also in the orchard, Brontë changes from retrospective narrative in the past tense

to a spontaneous present tense so that we can share Jane's feelings at the time. As the smell gets stronger she uses the strongest modal auxiliary verb to express the urgency in 'I must flee'. She does not explain why this governess needs to flee from her employer. He has not given her any indication that he is a threat, so presumably she is frightened of her own feelings.

Jane reverts to the past tense as she tells us what she remembers of her thoughts and describes her attempts to depart unnoticed. She still sounds surprised as she asks 'could his shadow feel?' The reader, however, is not surprised as Brontë has already suggested that he saw her from the library window. Perhaps Brontë wishes to suggest that Jane still cannot admit that deep down she hoped he would speak to her, which would have been impossibly forward for a governess in Victorian times.

Jane admits that she did 'not like to walk at this hour alone with Mr Rochester in the shadowy garden' She perceives it as a 'fault' in herself that she cannot always frame an excuse quickly. As a governess, she knows she is expected to remain in the background and not act as if she is her employer's equal, but she clearly wishes to stay and spend time with him and this is why she cannot make up a reason to depart. She seems torn between her feelings for him and what she sees as her duty. Clearly, at this point, because of the way in which her feelings have been heightened in the Romantic setting, she is unable to obey her reason, which tells her that there is no hope of marriage and any other liaison is quite out of the question. If she stays, however, she might give herself away, revealing her feelings to him, and make herself vulnerable. The 'evil' she speaks of cannot refer to Mr Rochester, as he has done nothing untoward, so she must be speaking of her own feelings. She calls them evil because her whole life she has been made aware that, as a woman and as a dependant, she must not show her feelings. Whenever she has lost control of her emotions previously in the novel, she has regretted it.

# The women in Mr Rochester's life: Chapter XXVII

On pp. 351–59 Mr Rochester tells Jane the details of his previous marriage and subsequent behaviour. Since he is our sole informant for much of his narrative, we have to accept it, but we can recognise the positive spin he puts on his story, trying to portray himself in an admirable light. He tells Jane, for instance, that Bertha's 'vices sprang up fast and rank: they were so strong, only cruelty could check them, and I would not use cruelty'. And yet he imprisons her in a room without a window, which is empty except for a fire and a lamp, for ten years of solitary confinement with nothing to do. It is hardly suprising that she resembles a caged animal by the time Jane hears and sees her.

One of the problems with a first-person narrative is that it is difficult for the writer to guide the reader's opinions. In this case the narrative is supposedly filtered through Jane's memory, but Jane loves Mr Rochester and wants to believe in him. Brontë, however, has allowed the facts to speak for themselves. He freely admits that he married Bertha for her money when he was 22, although he blames his father and brother, and, while he needed her money, he lived with her as man and wife. However, when his father died four years later, he was rich enough not to need her any more. He could not divorce her, so he locked her up.

On p. 358, he tells Jane: 'I tried dissipation — never debauchery: that I hated, and hate...That was my Indian Messalina's attribute...Any enjoyment that bordered on riot seemed to approach me to her and her vices, and I eschewed it.' The word 'dissipation' comes from a Latin word meaning 'to throw away' and is used to describe wasting one's life in the pursuit of pleasure, with connotations of being loose in morals and unrestrained in the pursuit of sensual gratification. The word 'debauchery' comes from Old French and means excessive sensual indulgence.

Mr Rochester implies that the two words have contrasting meanings and that his behaviour was less reprehensible than his wife's. However, the difference could simply be that, in nineteenth-century England, men were expected to enjoy sex and even to have mistresses, whereas women were not. The implication is that Bertha had lovers but after he left her at Thornfield he had a succession of foreign mistresses, whom he then discarded. Perhaps the clue to Mr Rochester's understanding of these words lies in the last sentence quoted above; 'riot' suggests that, while Bertha was unrestrained in her enjoyment of life, he expected her to behave like an Englishwoman, or in the manner in which Jane has been taught to behave. Mr Rochester discards his mistresses for various reasons: Céline Varens was unfaithful; 'Giacinta was unprincipled and violent', and 'Clara was honest and quiet; but heavy, mindless, and unimpressible'.

In the description Mr Rochester gives Jane of Bertha when he first met her, he compares her to Blanche Ingram (p. 352): 'Miss Mason was the boast of Spanish Town for her beauty: and this was no lie. I found her a fine woman, in the style of Blanche Ingram: tall, dark, and majestic.' As well as their appearance, there are a number of other similarities between Blanche and Bertha. Both women apparently treat their social inferiors badly: Blanche boasts about how she persecuted her governesses, and Mr Rochester tells Jane that 'no servant would bear the continued outbreaks of her [Bertha's] violent and unreasonable temper' (p. 353). We are told that both Blanche and Bertha have low intellects (pp. 215 and 353), and it seems that both women set out to seduce Mr Rochester. On p. 217, Jane observes that, if Blanche loved Mr Rochester, 'she need not coin her smiles so lavishly, flash her glances so unremittingly, manufacture airs so elaborate'. On p. 352, Mr Rochester describes how Bertha 'flattered me, and lavishly displayed for my pleasure her charms and accomplishments'.

Brontë may have chosen to make Blanche Ingram similar to Bertha in some respects because she wishes to explain why Mr Rochester felt no compunctions about trifling with Blanche's feelings in order to make Jane jealous. It could be that she wanted to show her readers how the young, inexperienced Mr Rochester would have been taken in by his bride's seductiveness, but it could just be that she wanted them both to appear to be a total contrast to Jane. If we look closely at Mr Rochester's speeches, we realise that he was attracted to Jane by her youth (Blanche is 25, Bertha is five years older than he), her quiet self-control, her intelligence, her reticence and the fact that she is unused to society.

Mr Rochester does not treat women with respect. Bertha, as we have seen, he married for money, lived with as man and wife until he inherited the estate, and then disposed of her in what he seems to think is a humane fashion. In Chapter XXVII, he tells Jane that he hates the time he spent in Europe: 'Hiring a mistress is the next worse thing to buying a slave.' However, this is evidence that he is self-centred, not that he is ashamed of the way he treated these women. He explains 'both are often by nature, and always by position, inferior: and to live familiarly with inferiors is degrading'. Blanche Ingram he has falsely courted and then discarded. Jane tells him (p. 303) 'It was a burning shame and a scandalous disgrace to act in that way. Did you think nothing of Miss Ingram's feelings, sir?' He replies, 'Her feelings are concentrated in one — pride; and that needs humbling.' Once again he uses a woman for his own purposes (to make Jane reveal her love for him out of jealousy), and in justifying his actions he reveals his misogyny in declaring that women should be humble.

He shamelessly manipulates Jane into declaring her passion for him. Once she has agreed to marry him he showers her with expensive clothes and jewels, and 'his smile was such as a sultan might, in a blissful and fond moment, bestow on a slave his gold and gems had enriched' (p. 310). Ironically, Mr Rochester himself brings about the destruction of his hopes of a bigamous marriage — it is because he treats Jane like a possession that she writes to her uncle in Madeira in the hope of a small inheritance to give her financial independence. On p. 349, after the revelation that Mr Rochester is already married, he assumes Jane will still live with him and, when she resists, he says 'Jane! Will you hear reason?...because, if you won't, I'll try violence.' He always expects women to give in to his demands and sees this as 'reasonable'. As Jane leaves Thornfield, he has made her feel guiltily that she is 'the instrument of evil' to the man she 'wholly' loves (p. 370). Even at the end, when she is financially independent, and he is physically dependent on her because he is blind and crippled, he still expects to own her completely. Jane 'meant to become her [Adèle's] governess once more, but I soon found this impracticable; my time and cares were now required by another — my husband needed them all' (p. 518).

# Critical responses: Chapter XXXIV

In order to ask Jane to marry him, St John invites her to take a walk with him. However, before they go, Brontë includes Jane's observations about the way she responds to 'positive, hard characters'. This reminds the readers of Jane's outbursts against John Reed and his mother. We recognise the appropriateness of her metaphorical comparison of her outbursts with a volcano: she has shared with us her seething passions, like molten lava ready to erupt when her tormentor goes too far. This seems like a melodramatic explanation of why she agreed to accompany St John on the walk, but Brontë's narrator, Jane Rochester, is speaking with hindsight, and she raises the reader's anticipation that there will be conflict.

Jane then describes the weather and the wild track of the glen through which they walk. This is a sensuous Romantic description in which we are invited to *feel* the gentle west breeze, *smell* the sweet scent of heath and rush, *hear* the swollen stream pouring down the ravine and *see* the bright colours sparkling like precious gems (sapphire and emerald), gleaming like rich gold or spangled like stars. We are made aware of Jane's love of nature, and Brontë is able to convey Jane's contented, even happy, mood, reminding us of her Romantic affinity with nature.

St John walks through this glen, apparently unaffected by its beauty. He stops by a 'battalion' of rocks, 'guarding' a pass. This military imagery suggests harshness and discipline. Jane continues to romanticise her description, personifying the mountain as having shaken off rich clothing and jewels, now having only 'heath for raiment and crag for gem'. No longer merely 'wild', the landscape is 'savage' and cruel, and the mood is 'frowning' rather than fresh. Jane sums up the place by saying that the rocks 'guarded the forlorn hope of solitude, and a last refuge for silence'. This is a place for the lonely to go to when all hope is lost and they need a last refuge. This hard, unforgiving landscape is an appropriate setting for St John to choose, since he has, with difficulty, suppressed all emotion and replaced it with reason and duty. Perhaps he needs this 'savage' landscape to prevent his resolve from softening. Jane, however, seems put on her guard by the harshness and it helps her to resist his proposal.

They sit down and St John says nothing for half an hour. Jane's observations of his actions and his words before the silence suggest that he may be repressing regret that he is to leave his beloved home. He removed his hat and 'let the breeze stir his hair and kiss his brow', like the touch of an affectionate woman. Always inclined to give supernatural explanations, Jane describes his silence as 'communion with the genius [spirit] of the haunt'. When he speaks, it is to console himself that he will see this (perhaps his favourite spot or perhaps the moors in general) in his dreams in India, and again when he sleeps 'on the shore of a darker stream'. This is clearly a reference to one of the rivers in classical mythology that separate this life from the next. St John is expecting to die in India, without ever returning home. Jane observes 'An austere patriot's passion for his fatherland!' In this half hour of silence, he seems to be fighting a passionate desire to stay and repressing his love of home.

As she counters his arguments that it is right for him to urge and exhort other people 'direct from God' to 'enlist under the same banner', she feels as if she is falling under a 'spell'. Jane often describes herself as bewitched. It seems to be her way of explaining when her feelings overwhelm her. In the red-room, for instance, the knowledge that Mr Reed died there cast a 'spell' on her as a child. Jane antici-pates St John's request, and her dread of his proposal is revealed in the words 'awful charm', 'trembled', 'fatal'. Once he has spoken, his words will 'rivet the spell', a metaphor that suggests that his words will fix the spell permanently, so she will have to agree. She describes feeling as if her 'iron shroud' contracted around her. A shroud is the cloth used to wrap the dead before they are buried, so clearly she expects the Indian climate to kill her, and iron is known for its strength, so she feels as if an external force is irresistible. Nevertheless, her desire to go with him comes from within.

St John has observed her for ten months, and he has seen the Jane she has learned to show to the world. She has managed to suppress her passions and to appear calm, controlled and dutiful. However, he has misunderstood her essential nature. When she split her inheritance and shared it with her cousins, he 'recognised a soul that revelled in the flame and excitement of sacrifice'. He has directed all his burning passions into self-sacrifice in the hope of glory, but Jane values love, a home and family above money or glory — it was no sacrifice for her. When he lists her qualities, they all agree with the reader's perception of her except the first one. We know that although she appears docile she is a fiercely independent woman who knows her own mind.

Feminist critics see much significance in Jane's response to his proposal. When St John first asks what her heart says, Jane repeats her answer as if desperate to stop him speaking the dreaded words. However, Brontë describes her as 'struck and thrilled', suggesting that the prospect of sacrificing herself as a missionary excites her. When he asks her to come as his 'helpmeet and fellow-labourer', 'the glen and sky spun round: the hills heaved', as if she nearly faints. Her ambition tells her that being a missionary is 'the most glorious man can adopt or God assign'. 'It was as if I had heard a summons from Heaven', she says, supporting her claim for equality on p. 129: 'Women are supposed to be very calm generally: but women feel just as men feel; they need exercise for their faculties, and a field for their efforts as much as their brothers do.' St John seems to offer her just what she wanted, however, as Gilbert and Gubar say: 'her progress towards selfhood will not be complete until she learns that "principle and law" in the abstract do not always coincide with the deepest principles and laws of her own being.' What St John offers would mean disowning half her nature. They conclude that 'despite the integrity of principle that distinguishes him from Brocklehurst...St John is finally, as Brocklehurst was, a pillar of patriarchy, "a cold cumbrous column"'.

Psychoanalytic critics read this novel as Charlotte Brontë's subconscious exploration of her relationship with her father. The male characters all try to dominate and control Jane, and she submits to their authority until they try to make her do something that is against her nature. Diane Sadoff sees *Jane Eyre* as a novel that allowed Brontë to understand, master, and free herself from her relationship with her own father.

Terry Eagleton, a Marxist critic, argues that:

> At the centre of all Charlotte's novels...is a figure who either lacks or deliberately cuts the bonds of kinship. This leaves the self a free, blank, 'pre-social' atom: free to be injured and exploited, but free also to progress, move through the class structure, choose and forge relationships, strenuously utilise its talents in scorn of autocracy or paternalism. The novels are deeply informed by this bourgeois ethic, but there is more to be said than that. For the social status finally achieved by the déraciné self is at once meritoriously won and inherently proper.

He notes that: 'Rivers is introduced into the novel just as Jane has made a painfully authentic self-sacrifice, in order to dramatise the dangers inherent in that virtue and so pave the way back to Rochester and life.' He explains that:

> Rivers is a spiritual bourgeois, eager to reap inexhaustible profits, unflaggingly devoted to the purchase of souls, his driving will, rigorous self-discipline and fear of emotional entanglements reveal well enough the analogy between Evangelical and entrepreneur...Indeed, Rivers himself candidly admits the connection, if not exactly in those terms. His evangelical zeal is a sublimation of thwarted worldly impulse (quotation from *Jane Eyre* p. 432).

Eagleton adds that:

> ...because Rivers forces Brocklehurst's ideology to a pitch of Romantic intensity, he seems to offer Jane a version of what she finally achieves with Rochester: a way of conforming to convention which at the same time draws you beyond it, gathers you into a fuller, finer self-realisation. The point is that such a resolution is available in India for Rivers, but not for Jane. Rivers the missionary is both martyr and hero; Jane would merely have been a martyr.

Elsie Michie, a post-colonial critic, explains: 'Colonial dominance was at once a civilising mission and a violent subjugating force.' Jane sees being a missionary as God's work and she anticipates 'noble cares and sublime results'. However, the extensive use of military imagery does suggest the 'violent subjugating force'. St John enlists her 'under His standard', and he prizes her 'as a soldier would a good weapon'. Jane speaks of his 'measured warrior march' and offers him 'a fellow-soldier's frankness'. Of St John, Michie writes:

Early characterised as the epitome of 'hardness and despotism', Rivers exemplifies the desire to redress the inequities of one's position that fuels the colonial enterprise…Though troubling at home, this ruthless, ambitious drive, once exorcised to India, allows Rivers to be described as 'firm, faithful and devoted, full of energy and zeal, and truth, he labours for his race; he clears their painful way to improvement' (p. 521).

# Different interpretations: Chapter XXXVIII

The final chapter acts as an epilogue. Jane is supposedly writing ten years after she arrived at Ferndean. It is interesting to analyse the language she uses to assess whether Brontë really wants us to believe that Jane has now found what she wanted and feels that she has made the right choices in her life.

Jane tells her readers, in superlatives, that she knows 'what it is to live entirely for and with what I love best on earth. I hold myself supremely blest' and that, when he was blind, Mr Rochester 'loved me so truly, that he knew no reluctance in profiting by my attendance'. Three times she emphatically declares 'never did I weary' of doing things for him when he could not see. However, while he loved her 'truly', she loved him 'fondly'. Not only is she writing in the past tense when only ten years into their marriage, but 'fondly' sounds cooler than 'truly'. She says 'All my confidence is bestowed on him, all his confidence is devoted to me'; once again 'bestowed' sounds much cooler and more distant than 'devoted', as if her confidence is given as a gift. Her choice of language suggests that perhaps she does not love him quite as deeply as he loves her.

On p. 129, Brontë tells the reader that:

> Women are supposed to be very calm generally: but women feel just as men feel; they need exercise for their faculties, and a field for their efforts as much as their brothers do; they suffer from too rigid a restraint, too absolute a stagnation, precisely as men would suffer; and it is narrow-minded in their more privileged fellow-creatures to say that they ought to confine themselves to making puddings and knitting stockings, to playing on the piano and embroidering bags.

Jane is married when she writes this, which suggests that Brontë may not have been happy with the ending of this novel. Jane may not feel as 'supremely blest' as she professes. Indeed, when they married, Jane wanted to 'become her [Adèle's] governess once more', but 'my time and cares were now required by another — my husband needed them all'. Her time and cares are not freely given but 'required' by her husband, leaving her no opportunity to fulfil herself as a teacher. The woman who declared to Mr Rochester in Chapter XXIII (p. 293): 'I am no bird and no net ensnares me; I am a free human being with an independent will' is now 'bone of his bone, and flesh of his flesh'. This metaphor suggests that not only her body but also her independence and individuality have been entirely taken over by her husband.

Brontë has chosen to end Jane's autobiography with a eulogy of St John Rivers. When Jane was asked by St John to go to India with him as a missionary, she considered that, as Rochester was lost to her, this occupation was 'truly the most glorious man can adopt or God assign' (p. 466). She wrote of its 'noble cares and sublime results', but, although tempted to go, she realised that he did not love her and 'if I join St John, I abandon half myself'. St John recognised that 'though you have a man's vigorous brain, you have a woman's heart' and in the nineteenth century it was even more difficult than it is now for a woman to devote herself to both a career and a family. Jane chose love over intellectual fulfilment, but, as she recognised, by doing so she abandoned the half of her that sought a vocation. As she supposedly writes her autobiography, Jane Rochester considers that 'To have yielded then [to Rochester] would have been an error of principle; to have yielded now would have been an error of judgment' (p. 482).

When she realises from his letters that St John is dying, she seems overwhelmed with admiration for the 'resolute, indefatigable pioneer', 'firm, faithful and devoted, full of energy, and zeal, and truth, he labours for his race; he clears their painful way to improvement'. He may be dying unnaturally young, but, although she wept for this, his last letter 'filled my heart with divine joy'. Her adulation of him has not dimmed, but she admits to no regrets. Jane has always had a strong will to live, unlike Helen Burns, and to have gone with him would have been to sacrifice not only half herself but her life also.

Different readers respond in various ways to the end of this novel. You may think that Brontë compromises her principles when she maims and blinds Mr Rochester and gives Jane an inheritance in order to create, for Jane, the equality she has demanded throughout. However, it could be argued that they are now equal, not because Mr Rochester is weaker and Jane richer, but because both have come to know themselves more fully. Jane has achieved autonomy, not in gaining an inheritance, but in learning how to balance the different sides of her character. What Jane has been searching for is a home, and, with Mr Rochester, she says:

> I was at perfect ease because I knew I suited him: all I said or did seemed either
> to console or revive him. Delightful consciousness! It brought to life and light
> my whole nature: in his presence I thoroughly lived; and he lived in mine.

You may think that Brontë compromises her principles because Jane finds happiness only through marriage. However, Jane has strong religious principles as well as strong passions, so it is only in marriage that she can be completely fulfilled. She may seem to have abandoned her intellectual aspirations, but she has directed her talents into writing her autobiography.

Perhaps Brontë should not have engineered a happy ending, but it was not her intention to write a tragedy. The novel is morally uplifting because it demonstrates that a woman does not have to compromise her principles to find happiness. Jane has refused to bend to class prejudice and to gender prejudice, she has refused to allow herself to be pushed in directions that go against her nature, and she has demonstrated that a woman's quest for love need not stifle her intellectual, spiritual and emotional independence.

# Place names

As in the allegorical *The Pilgrim's Progress*, Charlotte Brontë has used significant place names. They are all compound words with appropriate associations and/or metaphorical meanings.

Jane's journey begins when she resists the oppression of her male cousin and speaks out against injustice; the image of **Gateshead** suggests that it is her mind that is confined. Metaphorically, the gate is shut, but Mr Lloyd opens it, and she can start on her journey.

**Lowood** is an appropriate name both because it is literally low, built in a 'cradle of fog and fog-bred pestilence', and because it is a place where the orphan daughters of impoverished gentlemen are prepared for their humiliating position in society. Just before Jane leaves, Bessie tells her 'You are genteel enough; you look like a lady', so, with Miss Temple as her role model, obviously the school has failed to humble her, although she has learned self-control.

When God expelled Adam and Eve from the Garden of Eden, he said: 'cursed is the ground for thy sake; in sorrow shalt thou eat of it all the days of thy life; thorns and thistles shall it bring forth to thee' (Genesis 3:17–18). Mr Rochester is being punished at **Thornfield** for his sins and Jane's self-control is tested in a number of ways on this field of thorns. There might even be an echo of the biblical 'crown of thorns'.

At **Marsh End**, 'Having crossed the marsh, I saw a trace of white over the moor'. She has escaped from the Slough of Despond, and she finds a family. The other name for the house is **Moor House**, where she experiences true freedom, symbolised by the moor.

By contrast, **Ferndean** is buried deep in a wood. As she approaches, it is like a labyrinth, 'so thick and dark grew the timber of the gloomy wood'. As in the fairy tale *Sleeping Beauty*, the trees were 'close-ranked' and 'all was interwoven stem, columnar trunk, dense summer foliage — no opening anywhere.' This symbolises the doubts and difficulties surrounding her quest, but, once she has penetrated the barrier, 'Fern' has positive associations with growth, gentle nature and the fresh, relaxing colour green. A dene is a narrow wooded valley, so the name not only describes the location but also implies that the place is natural, not shaped by man, as Jane says 'no flowers, no garden-beds'. Jane and her husband are secluded from society and can live according to their true natures.

# Character names

As with the buildings, Charlotte Brontë seems to have chosen the names of her characters carefully. There are frequently religious, mythical or historical associations. Some of them can be interpreted as metaphors, and Brontë also uses homophones, where words sound similar but have different spellings. Sometimes she chooses names that are deliberately similar to, or contrasting with, the names of other characters, and sometimes it is more fruitful to look at names in groups.

Jane's name reflects her looks and her character. She is 'plain Jane', with no pretensions and no social status. Her surname has a number of homophones. She is her uncle's 'heir', which gives her financial independence. She is often compared with spirits of the 'air'. She is tempted to 'err' and learns from her experiences. 'Ire' is an approximate homophone, which Brontë frequently uses — by Chapter XXXV Jane has learned not to attend to 'the suggestions of pride and ire', but they are still important factors in her personality. Mr Rochester addresses her as 'Miss Eyre' until she rescues him from the fire, and this marks a significant point in his feelings for her. He reverts to this formal mode of address when Jane makes him think she will marry St John Rivers in Chapter XXXVII.

In the seventeenth century, the Earl of Rochester was a brave soldier, brilliant satirist, and a libertine who despised society's attitude to sex. Brontë was probably thinking of him when she chose the name for her hero. It is significant that Jane refers to him as Mr Rochester throughout the novel, except for two references to 'my Edward' in the final chapter.

Brontë makes various parallels between the two families with whom Jane lives. Both families are related to Jane, the father is dead, there is one son and two daughters. Both family names begin with 'R' (Reed and Rivers), and both are associated with water. However, whereas reeds are weak and bend easily in the current, rivers flow strongly and purposefully; rivers bring life and it was in a river that the early disciples were baptised. The association of Rivers with baptism strengthens the contrast between St John and Mr Rochester, who undergoes a baptism of fire at Thornfield before he finds God. Choosing the same name for the sons emphasises the contrast: whereas John Reed is weak and amoral, St John, like his namesake, becomes a disciple, devoting his life to God's work. The name may have been suggested because Patrick Brontë studied at St John's College, Cambridge, which had strong evangelical connections. Diana, Roman goddess of chastity, and Mary, mother of Jesus, are names that suggest purity.

Miss Temple is Jane's first role model, and she provides a sanctuary for the orphan child. The religious associations of her name emphasise Jane's propensity for hero worship. She later admits 'I could not...see God for His creature [Mr Rochester]: of whom I had made an idol.'

Helen Burns's name strongly links her with the fire imagery of the novel. She burns with religious fervour, and there are signs that she also burns with indignation. Her dirty fingernails and untidy drawers suggest that she is also a rebel at heart. However, instead of struggling against injustice, she looks forward to death as a release from this life. On her tombstone is inscribed the word 'Resurgam', declaring that she will rise again, like a flame from the ashes.

It is also possible to find significance in some of the names for other minor characters. The plosive consonants in Mr Brocklehurst's name sound prickly and hard. Brock is a common name for a badger, which is fierce and tenacious. Blanche is French for white, with its connotations of coldness and lack of feeling. Rosamond comes from the Latin 'Rosa Mundi' meaning 'Rose of the World' and is clearly appropriate to someone who is not only beautiful, but also a very good person. Oliver suggests an olive branch, which is a biblical symbol of peace and, in classical mythology, sacred to Venus, goddess of love.

# The two Mrs Rochesters

Jane is a total contrast to both Blanche and Bertha in her youth, petite stature, and intelligence, but Brontë seems to have made her similar to Bertha in temperament. There are several references to Jane being 'mad' or unrestrained in the chapters that deal with her childhood:

- p. 15: 'like a mad cat'.
- p. 22: Mrs Reed 'sincerely looked on me as a compound of virulent passion, mean spirit, and dangerous duplicity'.
- p.34: Bessie 'proved beyond a doubt that I was the most wicked and abandoned child ever reared under a roof. I half believed her, for I felt, indeed, only bad feelings surging in my breast.'
- p. 44: 'Shaking from head to foot, thrilled with ungovernable excitement, I continued —'.
- p. 45: 'half an hour's silence and reflection had shown me the madness of my conduct...Something of vengeance I had tasted for the first time. As aromatic wine it seemed, on swallowing, warm and racy; its after-flavour, metallic and corroding, gave me a sensation as if I had been poisoned.'

At Gateshead, Jane learns by experience that losing her temper does not make her feel better, but it is at Lowood that she learns to control her passionate feelings.

- On p. 69, at Lowood, when Jane tells Helen that it is natural to resist those who punish her unjustly, Helen tells her that: 'Heathens and savage tribes hold that doctrine; but Christians and civilised nations disown it.'
- On p. 80, when humiliated by Mr Brocklehurst, she 'mastered the rising hysteria'.
- On p. 84, when she tells Miss Temple her story, she is 'mindful of Helen's warnings against the indulgence of resentment'.
- On p. 100, Jane tells her readers that from Miss Temple she had imbibed:

  ...something of her nature and much of her habits; more harmonious thoughts;
  what seemed better regulated feelings had become the inmates of my mind.
  I had given in allegiance to duty and order; I was quiet; I believed I was
  content: to the eyes of others, usually even to my own, I appeared a disciplined
  and subdued character.

When she goes to Thornfield, she appears quiet and self-disciplined, but her self-restraint is put to the test:

- On p. 216, Jane tells of her struggle with 'two tigers — jealousy and despair', at the prospect of Mr Rochester marrying Blanche Ingram. She manages to keep these tigers under control, but she is tested further.
- On p. 365, when she is torn between her love for Mr Rochester and her self-respect, she tells herself 'I will hold to the principles received by me when I was sane, and not mad — as I am now…They have a worth — so I have always believed; and if I cannot believe it now, it is because I am insane — quite insane, with my veins running fire, and my heart beating faster than I can count its throbs.'

Brontë shows her readers that Jane, like Bertha, is a passionate woman, but that, unlike Bertha, she learns to repress her feelings. Although Bertha appears to be just like a caged animal, Brontë does give hints of the unhappy woman who is not allowed a voice as outlined below.

## The laugh in the attic (p. 126)

The first mention of Bertha is at the end of Chapter XI. Jane hears a laugh, 'as tragic, as preternatural a laugh as any I ever heard' (p. 127). As well as using the adjective 'preternatural' to suggest something Gothic and beyond the range of nature, Jane also recognises the tragedy of the person laughing.

## The fire in the bedroom (Chapter XV)

Bertha escapes from her gaoler three times. The first time she sets Mr Rochester's bed alight. This event occurs during the night after Mr Rochester tells Jane about Céline Varens out in the garden. Bertha has no window, but Grace Poole may have told her. He speaks of his jealousy of Céline's other lover and perhaps jealousy also accounts for Bertha's actions.

Another interpretation could be that Bertha's fire is intended to be symbolic of Jane's own sexual desire, which Brontë could not overtly express. This tête-à-tête in the garden has kindled her love for him, 'his presence in a room was more cheering than the brightest fire', and perhaps the dousing of the fire in Mr Rochester's bedroom is a symbolic dousing of the fire of her dangerous passion.

## The attack on Mr Mason (Chapter XX)

The next time we hear of Bertha Mason, she has attacked her brother. Mr Mason tells Mr Rochester, 'she said she'd drain my heart', so she is not merely reacting like a wild animal. Her brother had been part of the conspiracy to marry her to a fortune hunter, and he seems to have done nothing to prevent her being taken to England and subjected to this degrading imprisonment.

Once again, this attack comes just after Jane and Mr Rochester have become more intimate after his impersonation of a gypsy. On p. 236, she admitted to him 'I'd give my life to serve you'. Once again her desire is breaking through the self-restraint. On p. 186, Jane had warned herself that:

> It does good to no woman to be flattered by her superior, who cannot possibly intend to marry her; and it is madness in all women to let a secret love kindle within them, which, if unreturned and unknown, must devour the life that feeds it.

Perhaps Bertha is intended to be a symbol of what happens to a woman if she allows her desire to control her.

## Tearing the veil (Chapter XXV)

The second time Bertha escapes, she rips Jane's wedding veil. It is significant that she does not try to harm Jane. Once again, her action does not seem to be mindless violence. Mr Rochester seems to fear Bertha's jealousy as he tells Jane (p. 329) 'there is room enough in Adèle's little bed for you. You must share it with her to-night'.

As Adèle slept, Jane 'watched the slumber of childhood — so tranquil, so passion-less, so innocent…She seemed the emblem of my past life; and he I was now to array myself to meet, the dread, but adored, type of my unknown future day'. So, just as Adèle represents her passionless past, perhaps Bertha represents her fears of her own sexual passion. When Jane looks in the mirror, she sees Bertha throw the veil over her own head. It seems that, by using the device of the mirror, Brontë is reinforcing the idea that Bertha is Jane's passionate, sexual, but necessarily hidden self.

## The wedding (Chapter XXVI)

When Bertha is finally revealed, she is introduced by Mr Rochester as 'bad, mad and embruted'. Women who displayed a sexual appetite were considered to be no better than animals. We can only speculate how far Brontë intends us to believe that she has been turned into a brute by her mental illness and how far by the brutalising treatment she has suffered in 15 years of marriage.

Jane describes her as 'like some strange wild animal' and as a 'clothed hyena'. However, we are reminded that Jane is a biased narrator when she writes, in an admiring tone: 'He could have settled her with a well-planted blow; but he would not strike; he would only wrestle.' Bertha is bound to a chair, treatment that reminds the reader of Jane's own humiliation when she was locked in the red-room. Because she struggled, Bessie and Miss Abbot prepared to tie her to the chair, and 'This preparation for bonds, and the additional ignominy it inferred, took a little of the excitement out of me' (p. 15). This echo of Jane's own vain struggles against oppression acts as a reminder of the similarities between the two characters.

## Thornfield on fire (Chapter XXXVI)

Two months after Jane left, Bertha escaped from her prison for the last time. 'She set fire first to the hangings of the room next her own, and then she got down to a lower story, and made her way to the chamber that had been the governess's…and she kindled the bed there' (p. 492). She then climbed to the roof, 'where she was standing, waving her arms above the battlements, and shouting out till they could hear her a mile off'. As Mr Rochester approached, 'she yelled and gave a spring, and the next minute she lay smashed on the pavement' (p. 493).

Despair not madness may have led Bertha to set fire to the hangings in her gaoler's room, then seek out her rival's room and set fire to that, then to climb to the roof and throw herself to her death.

At the time this happens, Jane has settled into her new life as village school-mistress and she observes 'compared with that of a governess in a rich house, it was independent' (Chapter XXX). Her passionate feelings for Mr Rochester have been firmly suppressed. However, Brontë reminds us of Bertha and the way she has been treated when Jane tells St John Rivers, on p. 428, 'solitude is at least as bad for you as it is for me'.

# Edward Rochester and St John Rivers

Charlotte Brontë was an avid reader of Lord Byron's poetry, and she became fascinated by his male heroes. Particularly in the following poems: 'Lara', 'Manfred', 'The Corsair', and 'Childe Harold's Pilgrimage', Byron's heroes seem to be largely based on himself. Brontë's depiction of Mr Rochester owes a substantial debt to the Byronic hero. Stephen Coote, in his biography *Byron: The Making of a Myth*, writes:

> The Byronic hero was to have a profound influence on the European Romantic movement…Isolation, mystery, and hatred of mankind mingle with appearances of conviviality, and even mirth. The Byronic hero is cynical, soft-hearted, and

corrupted by secret guilt, yet he somehow preserves the traces of a noble spirit and even the ability to inspire love (sections 17, 18, and 19 from 'Lara'). Culled from Milton, Rousseau, Goethe and Schiller, the Byronic hero was mixed with a little of the villains of the popular thriller writer Mrs Radcliffe and much of Byron's own moods. Under whatever name he happens to go… the Byronic hero of this period is a fiery and lawless outsider, smitten with melancholy, burning with remorse, and activated by fierce political passions. He lives in the outer reaches of exotic and distant countries and, having either saved his women or condemned them to horrible punishments, found revenge or been revenged upon, he dies as a monk or a freedom fighter.

Through Mr Rochester's own words, Brontë reveals that his present personality is shaped by past events. On p. 155, Mr Rochester tells Jane:

No, young lady, I am not a general philanthropist; but I bear a conscience… When I was as old as you, I was a feeling fellow enough; partial to the unfledged, unfostered, and unlucky; but Fortune has knocked me about since: she has even kneaded me with her knuckles, and now I flatter myself I am as hard and tough as an India-rubber ball.

Cynically he comments: 'Most things free-born will submit to anything for a salary.' He admits that: 'I have a past existence, a series of deeds, a colour of life to contemplate within my own breast' and tries to excuse his guilty secret:

I started, or rather…was thrust, on to a wrong tack, at the age of one-and-twenty, and have never recovered the right course since; but I might have been very different; I might have been as good as you — wiser — almost as stainless…Nature meant me to be, on the whole, a good man… (pp. 158–59).

But he is clearly burning with remorse:

When fate wronged me, I had not the wisdom to remain cool: I turned desperate; then I degenerated…I wish I had stood firm — God knows I do! Dread remorse when you are tempted to err, Miss Eyre; remorse is the poison of life.

Smitten with melancholy he moans: 'I could reform — I have strength yet for that — if — but where is the use of thinking it, hampered, burdened, cursed as I am?' We learn in Chapter XV, that Jane believed this as she remembers:

I believed that his moodiness, his harshness, and his former faults of morality… had their source in some cruel cross of fate. I believed he was naturally a man of better tendencies, higher principles, and purer tastes than such as circumstances had developed, education instilled, or destiny encouraged (p. 172).

However, Brontë does not make him conform completely to her models. On his first appearance, he certainly looks the part. He is mounted on a 'tall steed' and accompanied by a 'great dog', both suggesting male virility and associated in Jane's mind with the mysterious Gytrash. However, Brontë immediately breaks the mould and makes him fall from his horse. He loses his dignity and is forced to rely on Jane for help. This signals that Brontë's treatment of her Byronic hero may not be entirely admiring.

In Chapter XIV, Jane starts to warn this 'fiery and lawless outsider' against defying the laws of God and man. When he declares 'I have a right to get pleasure out of life: and I *will* get it, cost what it may', she replies 'Then you will degenerate still more, sir' (p. 160). When he declares 'I know what my aim is, what my motives are; and at this moment I pass a law, unalterable as that of the Medes and Persians, that both are right', Jane contradicts him: 'They cannot be, sir, if they require a new statute to legalise them.' Through their conversations, Brontë explores and condemns the ideas of individualism and self-determination represented by Byron's heroes.

In Chapter XXVII, we learn what Mr Rochester's 'secret guilt' actually is. Everything stems from his lack of judgement in allowing himself to be rushed into marriage because he 'was dazzled, stimulated: [his] senses were excited' and 'competitors piqued' him (p. 352). He lost his independence, his freedom to decide his own future and his self-respect. He tells Jane 'I have no respect for myself when I think of that act! — an agony of inward contempt masters me.' Clearly, Brontë does not approve of his behaviour.

Like Byron's heroes he accepts responsibility for his actions, bringing his wife with him to Thornfield instead of abandoning her in the West Indies, but he hides her away and attempts to deny the bond between them and to commit bigamy. When he is exposed, he says 'I am little better than a devil at this moment' (p. 336). Like Byron's heroes he has travelled restlessly to escape the past, but Brontë invites us to condemn his affairs when Jane responds: 'I don't like you so well as I have done sometimes, indeed, sir. Did it not seem to you in the least wrong to live in that way, first with one mistress and then another?' (p. 359).

He does not become a freedom fighter or a monk, although he does turn to God. He tells Jane in Chapter XXXVII, 'I supplicated God, that, if it seemed good to Him, I might soon be taken from this life, and admitted to that world to come, where there was still hope of rejoining Jane' (p. 515). Instead of perpetuating the philosophy of the Byronic hero, Brontë rewards her hero only after he gives up his determination to create his own future.

Contrastingly, Jane tells her readers that St John Rivers is like 'the warrior Greatheart, who guards his pilgrim convoy from the onslaught of Apollyon'. In *The Pilgrim's Progress*, Bunyan tells us that Apollyon was 'a foul fiend'. Like Mr Rochester, St John battles against 'foul fiends', but his are different. As a missionary, his hopes are 'of carrying knowledge into the realms of ignorance — of substituting peace for war, freedom for bondage, religion for superstition, the hope of heaven for the fear of hell' (p. 431), so his fiends are ignorance, war, bondage, superstition and fear. The demons he faces as a man are his worldly ambitions. A year before he met Jane he was 'intensely miserable' because he thought he had made a mistake in his choice of career. He tells her 'yes, the heart of a politician, of a soldier, of a votary of glory, a lover of renown, a luster after

power, beat under my curate's surplice' (p. 416). His hope is that being a missionary will satisfy these ambitions. He labours not for love of his fellow man but for the 'incorruptible crown' (p. 521).

In appearance the two men are a total contrast. St John is fair and exceptionally handsome, whereas Mr Rochester is dark and not at all good-looking. However, in many ways they are very similar. Both men are forceful and egotistical, totally confident in their own judgement. Mr Rochester thinks he can dictate what is right, and he refuses to sacrifice his chance of happiness. St John thinks he knows what God wants — he rejects love and sacrifices his life for what he believes. Both men try to dominate Jane and force her to do what they want against her own judgement.

Brontë uses Rosamond Oliver to point out the similarity between Jane and St John: 'good, clever, composed, and firm' (p. 425). St John appeals to that ambitious side of Jane's character that is drawn to 'the most glorious [occupation] that man can adopt or God assign' (p. 466). The fact that she ends her autobiography with a eulogy of St John shows how important ambition is to her, but this occupation is only 'the one best calculated to fill the void left by uptorn affections and demolished hopes'. Whereas St John offers duty, sacrifice and a place in heaven, Mr Rochester offers love and a home, both of which the orphan has craved throughout the book. She is only superficially similar to St John, whereas of Mr Rochester she says that she is 'bone of his bone and flesh of his flesh' (p. 519).

Like Mr Rochester, St John is also associated with fire, but, whereas Mr Rochester burns with sexual desire, St John burns with a desire for glory and power. He tells Jane that, a year earlier, he 'burnt for the more active life of the world' (p. 416). However, he has redirected these feelings into the service of God. He claims to have suppressed sexual desire, but admits to Jane that he loves Rosamond 'wildly' (p. 431), and when he looks at her portrait he gives in briefly to 'delirium and delusion' (p. 430). He tells Jane: 'I rested my temples on the breast of temptation…The pillow was burning', and he dismisses his feelings as 'a fever of the flesh'. He claims to be 'a cold hard man' because he thinks he has effectively repressed his natural feelings. On the surface he appears cold and so is often associated with images of snow and ice, or of stone.

On p. 471, when St John tells Jane: 'Refuse to be my wife, and you limit yourself for ever to a track of selfish ease and barren obscurity', this could be seen as foreshadowing the final chapter. Jane's life at Ferndean is, indeed, obscure, hidden away from society, and she gives up her aspirations and her restlessness to devote herself to her family. In his view this is selfish and will bring her no glory. However, he could be regarded as selfish for refusing to relinquish his plans, in spite of his sisters' entreaties and Rosamond's love for him. His repetition of the possessive pronoun signals his egotism when he says: 'Relinquish! What! my vocation? My great work? My foundation laid on earth for a mansion in heaven?

My hopes of being numbered in the band who have merged all ambitions in the glorious one of bettering their race' (p. 431).

# The influence of Romanticism

The Romantic movement of the eighteenth and nineteenth centuries has already been discussed on pp. 35–37. There is a substantial amount of evidence that Brontë was strongly influenced by her reading of Romantic thinkers. Below is a list of their beliefs, followed by just some of the evidence from the text of *Jane Eyre*.

**(1)** The human mind is a complex and profound entity: a living, changing, mysterious organism whose most valuable powers are its imagination and creativity:
- p. 215: Blanche was 'too inferior' to excite jealousy; 'her mind was poor, her heart barren by nature: nothing bloomed spontaneously on that soil'.

**(2)** They believed that the irrational and unknowable parts of the subconscious human mind are the source of the artistic drive:
- p. 147: Jane, speaking of her paintings: 'I saw them with the spiritual eye, before I attempted to embody them.'
- p. 148: Rochester notes that Jane 'did exist in a kind of artist's dreamland while you blent and arranged these strange tints'.

**(3)** Writers and artists have visions and aspirations beyond those of ordinary people, but they are unable fully to express themselves in their writing or art:
- p. 147: Jane says of her paintings: 'my hand would not second my fancy, and in each case it had wrought out but a pale portrait of the thing I had conceived.'
- p. 148: Jane 'was tormented by the contrast between my idea and my handiwork:… I had imagined something which I was quite powerless to realise'.

**(4)** A writer can never be completely at home in the physical universe but will be continually aspiring after eternity:
- p. 482: 'Religion called — Angels beckoned — God commanded — life rolled together like a scroll — death's gates opening, showed eternity beyond.'

**(5)** Human experience is too complex and profound to be fully understood. The soul is all important:
- p. 292: Jane tells Rochester: 'I have as much soul as you — and full as much heart!'
- p. 486: After she hears Rochester's voice, she feels that 'the doors of the soul's cell' had been opened; 'it had wakened it out of its sleep'.

**(6)** Reason is inadequate by itself; it must be tempered with feeling. The head should follow the heart:
- p. 432: St John declares: 'Reason, and not feeling, is my guide.'
- p. 479: Jane says: 'he forgets, pitilessly, the feelings and claims of little people.'
- p. 272: 'Feeling without judgment is a washy draught indeed; but judgment untempered by feeling is too bitter.'

(7) Inspired moments cannot be summoned at will. They come unbidden, but the presence of nature is important:

- p. 483: The room is full of moonlight when Jane hears Rochester's voice. She runs into the garden and declares that 'it is the work of nature'.

(8) Nature has a personality — she has human moods and moral impulses. She is consoling, guiding and morally uplifting. There is a temptation to worship nature:

- p. 372: 'I have no relative but the universal mother, Nature: I will seek her breast and ask repose.'
- p. 204: Jane sees the necessity to conceal her feelings for Mr Rochester as 'Blasphemy against nature!'

(9) Imagery, usually natural or exotic, is valued as a way of suggesting ideas rather than stating them directly:

- p. 295: 'The moon [Diana, goddess of chastity] was not yet set', when Rochester defies God and asks Jane to marry him. A thunderstorm suddenly erupts.
- p. 516: Mr Rochester says: 'I humbly entreat my Redeemer to give me strength to lead henceforth a purer life.'

(10) Romantic writing should be morally uplifting, by example or by exposing hypocrisy. Established religion should not support the social structures that oppress ordinary people:

- p. 75: Mr Brocklehurst: 'When you put bread and cheese, instead of burnt porridge, into these children's mouths, you may indeed feed their vile bodies, but you little think how you starve their immortal souls.'

(11) That which is inherent and original in man is natural. Children are naturally good and innocent. Civilisation and institutionalised life corrupt them:

- On the first page, Jane is already 'humbled by the consciousness of my physical inferiority'.
- p. 76: when he orders Julia's curly hair to be cut off, Mr Brocklehurst declares 'we are not to conform to nature'.

(12) Every individual has the same rights. The established social and political structures need to change to uphold these rights:

- p. 292: Jane tells Rochester: 'I am not talking to you now through the medium of custom, conventionalities…it is my spirit that addresses your spirit…equal.'
- p. 413: '…these coarsely-clad little peasants are of flesh and blood as good as the scions of gentlest genealogy.'

# Timeline

## Age 10

| | | |
|---|---|---|
| November | Jane resists John's tyranny. | Cold, wet weather reinforces Jane's isolation and the coldness of the Reed family towards Jane. |
| January | Jane is sent to Lowood. | Wintry weather reflects Jane's unhappiness at first and exacerbates the harsh living conditions. |
| April | Girls allowed country walks. | As Jane begins to flourish at school, spring comes. The warmer weather reflects her rising spirits. |
| May | Typhus. | The warmer weather brings typhus, which leads to improved living conditions. |
| June | Helen dies. | |

## Age 18

| | | |
|---|---|---|
| August | Miss Temple marries. | |
| September | Jane advertises. | |
| October | Jane goes to Thornfield. | Jane arrives on a cold, raw day, enhancing her feelings of isolation. Her rising spirits are reflected in the next day's sunshine. |
| January | Mr Rochester arrives. | After three months of winter, Jane is restless and goes out. Mr Rochester's horse slips because of ice on the road. |
| March | Fire in Rochester's bedroom. | |
| April | House party guests arrive. | A mild spring reflects the mood of the party and enhances Jane's jealousy. |
| | Mr Mason visits. | A romantic sunrise enhances the mood as Jane and Mr Rochester talk after Mason's departure |
| May | Mrs Reed dies. | Strong winds and heavy rain reflect Jane's turbulent feelings. |
| June | Jane returns to Thornfield. | A golden sunset creates a romantic atmosphere as Jane meets Mr Rochester. |
| Midsummer | Declarations of love. | A brilliant sunset enhances the romantic mood, but a sudden thunderstorm suggests impending catastrophe. |

| | | |
|---|---|---|
| | Jane writes to her uncle. | Lovely weather reflects Jane's happiness. |
| July | Bertha tears Jane's veil. | Another storm reflects Jane's anxiety. |
| | Mr Rochester returns. | Mr Rochester calms Jane's fears and the storm abates. |
| | Wedding day. | |
| | Flight. | Jane is too distraught to notice the lovely weather. |
| | Jane is alone on the moor. | The weather deteriorates as she grows hungry and weak. |
| August to September | Jane lives at Moor House. St John hears of uncle's death. Diana and Mary leave. Jane moves into the school. | Mild, summer weather enhances the attraction of the moors and her hosts. |
| | Thornfield burns down. | |
| December | Jane learns of her inheritance. | Snowdrifts have made the road impassable, so she knows St John's visit is significant. |
| | The family are reunited. | Christmas enhances Jane's joy at having a family at last. |
| May | St John's first proposal. | A romantic description of the fine May day makes St John's proposal seem even colder. |
| 1 June | Jane returns to Thornfield. | The weather is ominously overcast, wet and chilly. |
| | She goes to Ferndean. | Her anxious arrival is on a 'sad' cold wet evening, but next morning is optimistically bright and sunny. |
| 20 June | St John sails for India. | |
| **10 years later** | Jane writes her auto-biography. | 'Never did I weary of gazing for his behalf, and of putting into words, the effect of field, tree, town, river, cloud, sunbeam — of the landscape before us, of the weather round us.' |

# Imagery

## Metaphors from the weather

The novel uses imagery associated with the weather and the seasons to further the action or enhance the mood of the novel. As well as using weather literally, however, it is used figuratively in similes and metaphors. Here are a few examples with explanations:

(1) On p. 316 Jane admits: 'He [Mr Rochester] stood between me and every thought of religion, as an eclipse intervenes between man and the broad sun.'

Just as in an eclipse the moon prevents people seeing the sun, so Jane's love for Mr Rochester was so great that it stood between her and God. Brontë uses this image to show that Jane loved him too much. She needed to stop making an 'idol' of the man, so that she could give God his rightful place.

(2) On p. 341 Jane writes: 'A Christmas frost had come at midsummer; a white December storm had whirled over June.'

Just as a winter storm will destroy all the signs of summer, so the news of Mr Rochester's previous marriage had, in a sudden blast, destroyed all Jane's hopes of happiness. Once again, Jane is out in the cold, as she had been at Gateshead and at Lowood.

(3) On p. 417 'Mr Rivers had started at the first of those musical accents, as if a thunderbolt had split a cloud over his head'.

This image reveals how deep and strong are St John's feelings for Rosamond Oliver, as he is unable to control his reactions when he hears her voice. The thunderbolt suggests the hot passion that lies beneath his reserve and apparent coldness.

## Images of ice and snow

Ice and snow are images frequently used both literally and figuratively in the novel.

(1) When Jane is looking at Bewick's *History of British Birds* (p. 10), she remembers particularly the bleak, cold vignettes that tell stories of death and disaster rather than the pretty or amusing ones. The cold, desolate images reflect her isolation at Gateshead and the lack of warmth in the family, but they also suggest that she is a strange little girl who seeks out images of death and disaster. Brontë uses these images to help us understand that it is not merely Jane's poverty that sets her apart from the family, but also her temperament.

(2) Both Mrs Reed and St John Rivers are frequently associated with ice, for instance:
(a) On p. 44 Mrs Reed's 'eye of ice continued to dwell freezingly' on Jane.
(b) On p. 511 Jane tells Mr Rochester that St John Rivers is 'good and great, but severe; and, for me, cold as an iceberg'.

## Fire and ice

As well as ice, fire also appears both literally and figuratively in the novel, and sometimes Brontë juxtaposes these two extremes. For instance, on p. 443 Jane and St John Rivers are talking: 'And then, he [St John] pursued, "I am cold: no fervour infects me."'

'"Whereas I [Jane] am hot, and fire dissolves ice."'

St John has tried to suppress his passions and become icily impervious to passion or persuasion. Jane recognises that his coldness is only assumed and that if she is persistent he will give her an answer. However, Brontë uses these recurring images to reinforce the contrast between them and how wrong it would be for Jane to marry St John. As Jane says 'as his wife…forced to keep the fire of my nature continually low, to compel it to burn inwardly and never utter a cry, though the imprisoned flame consumed vital after vital — *this* would be unendurable' (p. 470).

## Fire

Bertha is the character most obviously associated with fire, as she sets fire to Mr Rochester's bed and later to Thornfield itself. However, Jane is also frequently associated metaphorically with images of fire and burning. As well as the example above, on p. 45 Jane writes: 'A ridge of lighted heath, alive, glancing, devouring, would have been a meet emblem of my mind', and on p. 88: 'The fury of which she [Helen] was incapable had been burning in my soul all day.'

There are also many references that metaphorically associate Mr Rochester with fire. On p. 177, after Jane saves him from being burnt in his bed, she observes: 'Strange energy was in his voice, strange fire in his look.' On p. 365, after Jane refuses to stay with him: 'He seemed to devour me with his flaming glance: physically, I felt, at the moment, powerless as stubble exposed to the draught and glow of a furnace.'

## Pillars and columns

Several times Mr Brocklehurst is compared with a statue, a pillar or a column, reinforcing the impression that he is cold and unfeeling. St John Rivers is also compared with a statue and a column, but he tells Jane that, a year before, he 'burnt for the more active life of the world' (p. 416) and, when he saw Rosamond Oliver, Jane saw 'his solemn eye melt with sudden fire and flicker with resistless emotion' (p. 420). By using this contrasting imagery, Brontë is showing her readers that, although Jane and St John appear to be opposites, they both burn with inner desires. The difference is that, whereas for Jane human love is essential, St John is determined to live by 'Reason, and not feeling'. Nevertheless, Jane is strongly tempted by the sacrifice St John demands, and she declares: '…if I *do* make the sacrifice he urges, I will make it absolutely: I will throw all on the altar — heart, vitals, the entire victim', as he has done (p. 466).

Miss Temple is also linked with marble on p. 75, when Jane observes that, as Mr Brocklehurst spoke, 'her face, naturally pale as marble, appeared to be assuming also the coldness and fixity of that material; especially her mouth, closed as if it would have required a sculptor's chisel to open it'. Clearly Miss Temple is outraged at Mr Brocklehurst's words, but, unlike Jane, she will never voice her anger. She has repressed her passions and become a sanctuary, a 'temple' to whom Jane can go for understanding and sympathy.

## Birds

In contrast to these images of hard, cold stone, Jane and Mr Rochester are both compared with birds. On p. 314, Jane notices Mr Rochester's 'full falcon-eye flashing', and, at Ferndean, she notes that 'in his countenance I saw a change: that looked desperate and brooding — that reminded me of some wronged and fettered wild beast or bird, dangerous to approach in his sullen woe. The caged eagle, whose gold-ringed eyes cruelty has extinguished, might look as looked that sightless Samson' (p. 497). A few pages later, she uses the same image: 'The water stood in my eyes to hear this avowal of his dependence; just as if a royal eagle, chained to a perch, should be forced to entreat a sparrow to become its purveyor' (p. 507). To Jane, Mr Rochester seems like a noble bird, powerful, dominant and fierce. The reader will extend this comparison, noting that falcons and eagles are ruthless predators that have no pity for their victims. After the destruction of Thornfield, his injuries and his angry frustration make him seem like an eagle chafing at his captivity. He is now dependent on Jane.

Jane is always linked with small, insignificant-looking birds. As Mr Rochester describes his feelings when he first saw her, he compares her with a nimble, fragile-looking, but courageous linnet: 'It seemed as if a linnet had hopped to my foot and proposed to bear me on its tiny wing' (p. 360). At Ferndean, he cannot see her, just as it is often impossible to locate the singer when we hear a skylark, a bird that looks quite insignificant, but which has the most beautiful song, which it delivers so high in the sky that people can barely see it. 'Oh, you are indeed there, my skylark!' (p. 506). By association, the reader gleans that Jane may seem fragile, but she is determined and her voice brings joy to the blinded Mr Rochester. Jane compares herself to a common sparrow, small, plain and ordinary, and this analogy reveals the importance she places on appearance and her awareness of her own plainness.

At particular times, Brontë extends this imagery and Mr Rochester compares Jane to a caged bird. Soon after they meet, he says: 'I see at intervals the glance of a curious sort of bird through the close-set bars of a cage: a vivid, restless, resolute captive is there; were it but free, it would soar cloud-high' (p. 162). Just before he proposes, he urges her: 'Jane, be still; don't struggle so, like a wild frantic bird that is rending its own plumage in its desperation.' Her reply

rejects the comparison: 'I am no bird; and no net ensnares me' (p. 293). After the broken wedding, when he is desperate for Jane to stay, the imagery suggests that he is contemplating rape:

> Consider that eye: consider the resolute, wild, free thing looking out of it,
> defying me, with, more than courage — with a stern triumph. Whatever I do
> with its cage, I cannot get at it — the savage, beautiful creature! If I tear, if
> I rend the slight prison, my outrage will only let the captive loose (p. 366).

Although to a twenty-first century reader this could refer to her body, it is more likely that Brontë meant that Mr Rochester recognises Jane's free spirit, which is enclosed within a cage of convention. Not only is she a woman, she is also a governess and so unable to speak her mind or fulfil her ambitions. The jealousy he has aroused in her reveals the depth of her feelings to him, but she is still unable to voice them and she can only declare her independence. By the time she learns of his previous marriage, the cage has become her protection, and it is her belief in her principles that prevents him from persuading her to stay.

To Jane, birds are symbolic. She uses them to explain her feelings at having to abandon Mr Rochester. When she hears birdsong on the moors, 'Birds began singing in brake and copse: birds were faithful to their mates; birds were emblems of love' (p. 369). She tells us that her heart, 'impotent as a bird with both wings broken…still quivered its shattered pinions in vain attempts to seek him' (p. 373). So to Jane a bird is a symbol of love in its constancy and her love in particular, because, just as a bird with broken wings cannot fly to its mate, Jane's principles will not allow her heart to seek out the man she loves.

# Symbolism

In literature, a symbol combines an image with a concept. We have seen, for instance, how Jane took the image of a bird and used it to explain the concept of love. Whenever we read a literary text, we bring our previous experience with us, so a writer knows that images will evoke particular associations in our minds. When Brontë uses imagery, she expects us already to have ideas about what these images represent. When the same or similar images are used frequently throughout the novel, they achieve a particular resonance and increase in power.

## Fire and ice/heat and cold

These opposing images are ones that Brontë frequently evokes. From previous reading experience, we may already be thinking that fire destroys, but it also purifies. We need fire for warmth and energy, but we also fear fire as an element we cannot always control. In mythology, the phoenix is a fabulous bird, rather like an eagle, which burns to death on a funeral pyre and is then reborn out of the ashes. The phoenix rising from the fire has become a symbol for resurrection. As far as emotions are concerned, fire is usually used to represent strong passions such as love, anger and ambition, which can get out of control.

Whereas fire is constantly changing and has no fixed form, ice is solid with a fixed shape, until it comes into contact with heat. Ice can also inflict burns, and it will destroy new life. However, it is generally used to represent coldness of heart, repressed emotions, hopelessness, loneliness and isolation.

The red-room and the drawing room at Thornfield Hall are both described as chilly through disuse, but they are kept clean for the absent master of the house. Both rooms have looped curtains, mirrors, ottomans and a pale marble mantelpiece; both rooms are furnished in crimson and white. Jane writes of a 'general blending of snow and fire' as she describes the drawing room at Thornfield, suggesting that here, too, she will feel strong passions and also desolation.

At Gateshead and Lowood, Jane's burning indignation and desire for love were met with cold repression, rejection and isolation. At Lowood she learned to suppress her inner fire, and she achieved a temperate harmony. At Thornfield, however, her passions are rekindled as she falls in love with Mr Rochester. After he confides in her about Adèle's past, Jane cannot sleep. She muses on the fact that he no longer takes 'fits of chilling hauteur' (p. 171), and that, for her, 'his presence in a room was more cheering than the brightest fire' (p. 172). While she lies thinking, she hears a 'vague murmur, peculiar and lugubrious', and, as her door was touched, 'I was chilled with fear.' Is it coincidence that, just as she is admitting to her growing passionate love for Mr Rochester, fire threatens to consume him? After she has doused the fire, 'Strange energy was in his voice, strange fire in his look'. By this time, however, Jane is 'cold' (p. 177). She admits to her feelings for him, but reason prevents her from imagining a fairy-tale happy ending: 'Sense would resist delirium: judgment would warn passion.'

Gradually, fire has come to represent 'delirium' and 'passion', while cold has come to represent 'sense' and 'judgement'. Both are elements of Jane's personality, and the main theme of the novel is how she learns to reconcile the two apparent opposites. Mr Rochester is 'Vulcan', the destructive god of fire (p. 509); St John is carefully controlled ice, declaring 'Reason, and not feeling, is my guide'. Jane chooses passion, but only when Mr Rochester has been through his ordeal by fire, as Thornfield burnt down, and he acknowledges 'the hand of God in my doom'. He has begun to 'experience remorse, repentance; the wish for reconcilement to my Maker'. Jane loves him more now that she can be 'really useful' to him, and so she has achieved that balance of passion and reason. She is no longer at risk of losing her individual identity in her overwhelming love.

## The horse-chestnut tree

Jane tells us of the great tree and how it is struck by lightning on the evening when Mr Rochester defies God and society to propose to her, but as she waits for him

anxiously after Bertha had torn her veil, Jane gives the chestnut tree a symbolic status that becomes more significant for the reader as events unfold:

> Descending the laurel walk, I faced the wreck of the chestnut-tree; it stood up, black and riven: the trunk, split down the centre, gasped ghastly. The cloven halves were not broken from each other, for the firm base and strong roots kept them unsundered below; though community of vitality was destroyed — the sap could flow no more: their great boughs on each side were dead, and next winter's tempest would be sure to fell one or both to earth: as yet, however, they might be said to form one tree — a ruin, but an entire ruin.

> 'You did right to hold fast to each other,' I said: as if the monster-splinters were living things, and could hear me. 'I think, scathed as you look, and charred and scorched, there must be a little sense of life in you yet, rising out of that adhesion at the faithful, honest roots' (p. 318).

Jane speaks to the two halves of the tree as if they are two people in a relationship. Blasted by lightning, 'the time of pleasure and love is over with you: but you are not desolate: each of you has a comrade to sympathise with him in his decay'. The fact that the tree was struck immediately after Mr Rochester declared 'God pardon me!…and man meddle not with me: I have her and will hold her' is an ill omen. The readers, although we do not know of Mr Rochester's secret, are given an uneasy feeling that their love is to be similarly blasted. When Jane speaks to the tree, it seems like a premonition that Jane and Mr Rochester are going to be violently split asunder, but they will remain joined at 'the faithful, honest roots'.

In the penultimate chapter, Brontë once again uses the tree as a symbol. On p. 512, Mr Rochester sadly says: 'I am no better than the old lightning-struck chestnut-tree in Thornfield orchard', but Jane is back with him. Like the tree, their relationship has a 'firm base and strong roots'. Jane responds with 'You are no ruin, sir — no lightning-struck tree: you are green and vigorous'. Her optimism is well founded as, in the final chapter, we learn that, ten years later, he has children who, like the plants around the tree, 'grow about your roots…and…lean towards you, and wind around you, because your strength offers them so safe a prop'.

## The moon

The moon is introduced casually at first, although at key moments in the novel. Jane frequently personifies it, and gradually it achieves a symbolic status. After she breaks from Mr Rochester, Jane has a dream of being in the red-room at Gateshead. The strange light that had frightened her as a child, precisely because it was not the moon, seemed to mount the wall and pause in the centre of the ceiling; 'the gleam was such as the moon imparts to vapours she is about to sever'. This time the light seems to become the moon, and Jane watches with anticipation, 'as though some word of doom were to be written on her disc'. However, in her dream, when the moon broke through the clouds, it has metamorphosed into a white human form that gazed on her and whispered in her heart, 'My daughter, flee temptation!' She answers 'Mother, I will' (p. 367).

It might be more appropriate to refer to the moon as a character rather than a symbol, as Jane always refers to it with the feminine pronouns 'she' and 'her'. It appears frequently at key points in the novel. The moon gives Jane light to dress by as she leaves Gateshead, and helps to comfort her after her humiliation by Mr Brocklehurst. Its light guides her to Miss Temple's room when Helen is ill. The moon 'was waxing bright' when Jane first met Mr Rochester, and she is 'not at all afraid of being out late when it is moonlight'. This supportive presence seems to take an active role when Mr Mason is attacked, as, even before he screams, Jane tells us she 'looked in at me' and 'her glorious gaze roused me' (p. 238).

The moon is present when the tree is struck by lightning, and it appears in the fissure created by the two halves of the tree as Jane speaks to them. This time the moon is disturbingly ominous, but Brontë has withheld the reason: 'her disc was blood-red and half overcast; she seemed to throw on me one bewildered, dreary glance, and buried herself again instantly' (p. 319). Eventually we learn that Jane is waiting for Mr Rochester to return so she can tell him about the night-time visitor who tore her wedding veil. Brontë has projected Jane's puzzlement and anxiety onto the moon, to create anticipation in the reader. Even before Bertha appeared, Jane had dreamt a prophetic dream that Thornfield was a ruin (p. 325), and she wandered there 'on a moonlight night' carrying a little unknown child that clung to her, almost strangling her, until she fell from the crumbling wall. (The child is another symbol, possibly of Jane's own past as an orphan, which she cannot leave behind until the 'Bertha' side of her personality falls and dies.)

Jane sees the moon as a support, someone who advises her wisely. In the passage referred to, it seems that the moon has become the mother she never had. Perhaps, however, the moon is, for Jane, the eye of 'the universal mother, Nature' (p. 372). As she settles to sleep on the moors after fleeing from Thornfield, Jane rises to her knees to pray: 'Night was come, and her planets were risen' (p. 373). Her fears are calmed, and she feels safe. She has a strong awareness of God, 'and it is in the unclouded night sky, where His worlds wheel their silent course, that we read clearest His infinitude'. Brontë seems to suggest that perhaps the moon is more than a recurring motif because Jane sees it as the visible symbol of God's presence.

This attribution of human qualities to nature is often called the *pathetic fallacy*, the arousal of feeling by misleading means, after John Ruskin who coined the phrase to comment on 'the difference between the ordinary, proper, and true appearance of things to us; and the extraordinary, or false appearances, when we are under the influence of emotion, or contemplative fancy'. He criticised this kind of personification as 'morbid', but Brontë here shows how valuable a device it can be for revealing aspects of a character's personality, especially in a first-person narrative, and for heightening the dramatic tension.

# Themes

As a *Bildungsroman*, the main theme of *Jane Eyre* is Jane's growth to maturity and her struggle to attain self-fulfilment. She tells her story several times, to Mr Lloyd, Helen, Miss Temple, Mr Rochester, St John Rivers and finally to the readers of her autobiography. At first she struggles, because, as a child, she cannot analyse her feelings, but, ultimately, telling her story becomes her way of knowing herself and establishing her identity. Charlotte Brontë inevitably draws on themes of education, religion, gender equality, social class, and the need to love and be loved. As Jane journeys through life, she experiences many crises that force her into crucial judgements and decisions, both conscious and subconscious. By the end, she has learned to balance nature and nurture, and she has found lasting happiness.

The dramatic tension that makes the novel so powerful is created because Jane is frequently pulled in opposing directions. This means that it can be valuable to explore contrasting themes, although they are all interlinked and do not separate conveniently.

## Reason versus feeling

The supporting characters often embody one or other of these opposites, so St John consciously suppresses feeling and Mr Rochester considers what is reasonable to be what he feels is right. The two Reed sisters also are opposites: Georgiana embodies 'feeling without judgment' and Eliza 'judgment untempered by feeling'.

Jane is taught by experience to temper feeling with reason. When Mr Rochester attempts to persuade her to stay by telling her his story and speaking with contempt of his mistresses, she is able to balance her passionate love for him with rational thought. She realises that 'if I were so far to forget myself and all the teaching that had ever been instilled into me…he would one day regard me with the same feeling which now in his mind desecrated their memory' (p. 359).

## Rebellion versus conformity

From the beginning, Jane rebels against unjust authority, demands her rights as an equal, and demands liberty. Brontë, however, is concerned with individual battles and marginalises the struggles in society at large. Jane makes a sweeping reference to them on p. 129: 'Nobody knows how many rebellions besides political rebellions ferment in the masses of life which people earth.' This electrical image recognises the potentially explosive nature of the rebellions fermenting in society.

In the first chapters, Jane rebels against John Reed and his mother, but she finds that vengeance brings no lasting satisfaction: 'its after-flavour, metallic and corroding, gave me a sensation as if I had been poisoned' (p. 45). From Helen Burns, she learns the value of passive rebellion. Helen appears to submit to oppression and conform to society's expectations of a girl in a charity school.

However, when Miss Scatcherd beats her, she refuses to cry openly. Miss Scatcherd's response: 'Hardened girl!' reveals that she wanted to make Helen cry and probably inflicted more blows in an attempt to bring this about (p. 65).

Jane learns to mask her fiery, wilful, emotional nature under a coolly polite, submissive exterior. She has learned this lesson so well that she suffers greatly under Mr Rochester's tyrannical efforts to force her to show her feelings for him. She hides them until he threatens her independence, declaring that she must stay, even after he is married: 'I swear it — and the oath shall be kept' (p. 292).

Even after she has agreed to marry him, she still appears to conform to society's expectations of a submissive wife, but actually manages to control him. Mr Rochester observes:

> 'Jane, you please me, and you master me — you seem to submit, and I like the sense of pliancy you impart…I am influenced — conquered; and the influence is sweeter than I can express; and the conquest I undergo has a witchery beyond any triumph I can win' (p. 301).

## Duty versus inclination

In order to maintain her integrity and be true to her essential self, which she calls her 'soul', Jane has to learn not to follow her inclination but to listen to the voice of duty. When she decides to leave Thornfield, she personifies this internal battle: 'I wanted to be weak that I might avoid the awful passage of further suffering I saw laid out for me; and Conscience, turned tyrant, held Passion by the throat' (p. 343). When Mr Rochester begs her to stay, Jane describes her dilemma in terms of physical pain:

> I was experiencing an ordeal: a hand of fiery iron grasped my vitals. Terrible moment: full of struggle, blackness, burning!…him who thus loved me I absolutely worshipped: and I must renounce love and idol. One drear word comprised my intolerable duty — 'Depart!' (p. 363).

As she resists Mr Rochester's persuasion, she expresses this contrast in her character as one of the body versus the mind: '…physically, I felt, at the moment, powerless as stubble exposed to the draught and glow of a furnace: mentally, I still possessed my soul, and with it the certainty of ultimate safety' (p. 365).

Jane has another interesting struggle with duty versus inclination when she writes about teaching at Morton School: 'I felt — yes, idiot that I am — I felt degraded'; however, she anticipates a time when she will be able to 'substitute gratification for disgust' (p. 414).

## Earth versus heaven

Throughout the novel, Jane is presented with the dilemma of how to reconcile fulfilment in this life with a future in heaven. As a naïve ten-year-old, she tells Mr Brocklehurst that, to avoid going to hell she 'must keep in good health, and not die' (p. 39). At Lowood, Helen has abandoned hope of earthly fulfilment and set

her sights firmly on heaven: 'God waits only the separation of spirit from flesh to crown us with a full reward' (p. 83). St John also has rejected happiness in this life in favour of the next.

> St John...would have given the world to follow, recall, retain her [Rosamond], when she thus left him; but he would not give one chance of heaven, nor relinquish, for the elysium of her love, one hope of the true, eternal Paradise (p. 424).

Jane cannot accept Helen's abandonment of earthly love. Indeed she admits that, at Thornfield, her future husband became almost her hope of heaven and that she could not see God for his creature. She is tempted by St John's choice of self-sacrifice, but only because she has lost her hope of earthly happiness with Mr Rochester. She wonders:

> ...is not the occupation he now offers me truly the most glorious man can adopt or God assign? Is it not, by its noble cares and sublime results, the one best calculated to fill the void left by uptorn affections and demolished hopes...Alas! If I join St John, I abandon half myself (p. 466).

When she almost agrees to go with him to India as his wife, she acknowledges: 'I had now put love out of the question, and thought only of duty' (p. 482). She entreats heaven to show her the path, and that is when she has the strange psychic experience that calls her back to Mr Rochester. However, before she returns to him, she prays: 'I seemed to penetrate very near a Mighty Spirit; and my soul rushed out in gratitude at His feet' (p. 484).

Earlier in the novel, Mr Rochester sought salvation through Jane, now he has found it for himself. He only finds happiness on earth when he prays to God. He no longer tries to set his own laws and decide his own future — he accepts God's direction.

## Nature versus society

It is a central tenet of the Romantic movement that what is inherent and original in mankind is natural. Both man and nature are organic: they share a life force that allows them to develop and regenerate, as opposed to man-made worlds that cannot grow or reshape themselves. From the start of the novel, society is portrayed as at odds with nature. Society's artificial rules have marginalised Jane, because the family disowned her mother when she married beneath her. They forced Mr Rochester, a younger son, into a marriage of convenience and prevented him from divorcing Bertha when she went mad. They pushed the impoverished St John into a career in the church rather than letting him fulfil his worldly ambitions. He admits to 'the heart of a politician, of a soldier, of a votary of glory, a lover of renown, a luster after power'.

Jane has a passionate nature, which she must learn to control. Helen Burns tells Jane that, although it may be natural to resist those who punish her unjustly,

'Christians and civilised nations disown it'. Mr Brocklehurst declares: '…we are not to conform to nature. I wish these girls to be the children of Grace.' Victorian society regarded children as naturally bad and needing to be taught how to be good. By contrast, the Romantics, following Rousseau, regarded children as innocent and pure until corrupted by society. Brontë follows the Romantic view, but she does insist that following one's nature must be tempered by adherence to God's laws. When Mr Rochester, following the Romantic view that one may justifiably rebel against social conformity, asks Jane to 'transgress a mere human law' and stay with him, Jane determines to 'keep the law given by God'.

When Jane falls in love with her employer, she must deny her nature: 'He is not of your order: keep to your caste, and be too self-respecting to lavish the love of the whole heart, soul, and strength, where such a gift is not wanted and would be despised' (p. 189). She forbids herself to think of him except as her paymaster, but exclaims that this is 'Blasphemy against nature'. When Jane escapes from society onto the moors, she seeks refuge with 'the universal mother, Nature' and, when she hears Mr Rochester's voice, she is convinced that 'it is the work of Nature'. God's laws are not at odds with nature, but society's are.

It may be natural for Jane and Mr Rochester to marry, but Brontë does not try to reconcile the two opposing forces of nature and society. They live at Ferndean, secluded from society in a house that Mr Rochester thought too unhealthy for Bertha because of its 'ineligible and insalubrious site'. Jane has learned to reconcile her natural feelings with society's expectations, but Brontë is too much of a realist to imagine that society would change to accept her. There was no place in Victorian society for a marriage of equals.

# Useful quotations

The best quotations are those you have found useful in class discussions and practice essays, and they will require little conscious learning because you are already familiar with them. The most effective ones to learn in addition are those that serve more than one purpose, i.e. those that can be used to support a theme, image, or style usage, as well as a point about character or narrative effect. Consider each of the following quotations, as well as any favourites of your own, to decide how they could be used in exam essays or coursework.

## Chapter I

> Of these death-white realms I formed an idea of my own: shadowy, like all the half-comprehended notions that float dim through children's brains, but strangely impressive (Jane speaking of Bewick's *History of British Birds*)

## Chapter II

'You are less than a servant, for you do nothing for your keep' (Bessie to Jane)

'Unjust! — Unjust!' said my reason, forced by agonising stimulus into precocious though transitory power (Jane explaining her feelings as a child)

My heart beat thick, my head grew hot; a sound filled my ears, which I deemed the rushing of wings: something seemed near me; I was oppressed, suffocated: endurance broke down (Jane remembering how she felt in the red-room)

## Chapter III

*God is a friend to the poor orphan child* (Bessie's song: popular religion)

Children can feel, but they cannot analyse their feelings (Jane Rochester)

## Chapter IV

Human beings must love something (Jane Rochester)

Something of vengeance I had tasted for the first time. As aromatic wine it seemed, on swallowing, warm and racy; its after-flavour, metallic and corroding, gave me a sensation as if I had been poisoned (after Jane's outburst to her aunt)

## Chapter V

Breakfast was over and none had breakfasted (at Lowood, an antithetical statement)

## Chapter VI

'Yet it would be your duty to bear it, if you could not avoid it: it is weak and silly to say you *cannot bear* what it is your fate to be required to bear' (Helen to Jane)

## Chapter VII

'Naturally! Yes, but we are not to conform to nature' (Mr Brocklehurst)

'...my mission is to mortify in these girls the lusts of the flesh, to teach them to clothe themselves with shamefacedness and sobriety' (as above)

## Chapter VIII

'If all the world hated you, and believed you wicked, while your own conscience approved you, and absolved you for guilt, you would not be without friends' (Helen Burns to Jane)

'Hush, Jane! You think too much of the love of human beings' (as above)

'God waits only the separation of the spirit from flesh to crown us with a full reward' (as above)

## Chapter IX

Again I questioned; but this time only in thought. 'Where is that region? Does it exist?' (Jane after Helen has told her that she is sure she will go to heaven)

## Chapter X

I desired liberty…for liberty I uttered a prayer (when Miss Temple leaves)

'Then,' I cried, half desperate, 'grant me at least a new servitude!' (as above)

## Chapter XI

…the laugh was as tragic, as preternatural a laugh as any I ever heard (Jane has heard Bertha for the first time)

## Chapter XII

…restlessness was in my nature; it agitated me to pain sometimes (just before Mr Rochester arrives)

Millions are condemned to a stiller doom than mine, and millions are in revolt against their lot (as above)

Women are supposed to be very calm generally: but women feel just as men feel; they need exercise for their faculties, and a field for their efforts as much as their brothers do (as above)

It was an incident of no moment, no romance, no interest in a sense; yet it marked with a change one single hour of a monotonous life (after meeting Mr Rochester)

## Chapter XIII

'I was tormented by the contrast between my idea and my handiwork' (Jane tells Mr Rochester about her paintings)

## Chapter XIV

'I am not a general philanthropist; but I bear a conscience' (Mr Rochester to Jane)

'I should never mistake informality for insolence: one I rather like, the other nothing free-born would submit to, even for a salary' (Jane to Mr Rochester)

'Nature meant me to be, on the whole, a good man' (Mr Rochester to Jane)

'Dread remorse when you are tempted to err, Miss Eyre; remorse is the poison of life' (as above)

## Chapter XV

'…you will come some day to a craggy pass of the channel, where the whole of life's stream will be broken up into whirl and tumult, foam and noise' (as above)

I believed he was naturally a man of better tendencies, higher principles, and purer tastes than such as circumstances had developed, education instilled, or destiny encouraged (Mr Rochester has told Jane about his affair with Céline)

'I saw it in your eyes when I first beheld you: their expression and smile did not' — (again he stopped) — 'did not' (he proceeded hastily) 'strike delight to my very inmost heart so for nothing' (Mr Rochester to Jane after the fire in his room)

## Chapter XVI

It does good to no woman to be flattered by her superior, who cannot possibly intend to marry her; and it is madness in all women to let a secret love kindle within them (Jane when Mr Rochester has gone to a house party)

## Chapter XVII

'He is not of their kind. I believe he is of mine — I am sure he is — I feel akin to him' (Jane quotes her thoughts as she reflects on the difference in social status between her and Mr Rochester)

'Blasphemy against nature!' (Jane as she forbids herself to think of Mr Rochester except as her paymaster)

'…we are for ever sundered — and yet, while I breathe and think, I must love him' (as above)

## Chapter XVIII

…one vital struggle with two tigers — jealousy and despair (Jane thinks Mr Rochester will marry Blanche)

I thought only of my master and his future bride — saw only them, heard only their discourse, and considered only their movements of importance (as above)

## Chapter XIX

'Strong wind, earthquake-shock, and fire may pass by: but I shall follow the guiding of that still small voice which interprets the dictates of conscience' (after pretending to be a gypsy, Mr Rochester assesses Jane's character in her face)

'Can I help you, sir? — I'd give my life to serve you' (Jane after she tells him of Mr Mason's arrival)

## Chapter XX

'She sucked the blood! She said she'd drain my heart!' (Mr Mason of his sister)

'Sir…a wanderer's repose or a sinner's reformation should never depend on a fellow-creature' (Jane to Mr Rochester after Mr Mason's departure)

## Chapter XXI

Presentiments are strange things! And so are sympathies, and so are signs; and the three combined make one mystery to which humanity has not yet found the key (Jane philosophising when Robert arrives after she has a dream of a child, an ill omen)

I still felt as a wanderer on the face of the earth; but I experienced firmer trust in myself and my own powers, and less withering dread of oppression (Jane as she approaches Gateshead again)

…time quells the longings of vengeance and hushes the promptings of rage and aversion (Jane as she approaches Mrs Reed)

Feeling without judgment is a washy draught indeed; but judgment untempered by feeling is too bitter and husky a morsel for human deglutition (Jane judges her cousins, Georgiana and Eliza)

## Chapter XXII

'…wherever you are is my home — my only home' (Jane to Mr Rochester)

## Chapter XXIII

'I have talked, face to face, with what I reverence, with what I delight in — with an original, a vigorous, an expanded mind' (Jane to Mr Rochester)

'I am no bird; and no net ensnares me: I am a free human being with an independent will, which I now exert to leave you' (as above)

'My bride is here…because my equal is here, and my likeness' (Mr Rochester asks Jane to marry him)

'It will expiate at God's tribunal. I know my Maker sanctions what I do. For the world's judgment — I wash my hands thereof. For man's opinion — I defy it' (Mr Rochester defies God and man)

## Chapter XXIV

The feeling, the announcement sent through me, was something stronger than was consistent with joy — something that smote and stunned: it was, I think, almost fear (four weeks to the wedding day)

'Jane: you please me, and you master me' (Mr Rochester)

…the more he bought me, the more my cheek burned with a sense of annoyance and degradation (Jane and Rochester go shopping)

My future husband was becoming to me my whole world; and…almost my hope of heaven…I could not…see God for His creature: of whom I had made an idol (Jane realises the danger of her love for Mr Rochester)

## Chapter XXV

…the moon appeared momentarily…her disc was blood-red and half overcast; she seemed to throw on me one bewildered dreary glance (Jane waits to tell Mr Rochester of her night-time visitor)

## Chapter XXVI

…a figure ran backwards and forwards. What it was, whether beast or human being, one could not, at first sight, tell (in Bertha's attic room after the broken wedding)

He could have settled her with a well-planted blow; but he would not strike (as above)

A Christmas frost had come at midsummer (Jane retires to her room)

I lay faint; longing to be dead. One idea only still throbbed life-like within me — a remembrance of God (as above)

'...the waters came into my soul; I sank in deep mire: I felt no standing; I came into deep waters; the flood overflowed me' (as above: Jane quotes from the Psalms)

## Chapter XXVII

Conscience, turned tyrant, held Passion by the throat (Jane decides to leave)

I forgave him all: yet not in words, not outwardly; only at my heart's core (Mr Rochester has begged her forgiveness)

'Jane! Will you hear reason?...because, if you won't, I'll try violence' (he tries to force her to stay)

I was experiencing an ordeal: a hand of fiery iron grasped my vitals. Terrible moment: full of struggle, blackness, burning! Not a human being that ever lived could ever wish to be loved better than I was loved; and him who thus loved me I absolutely worshipped: and I must renounce love and idol. One drear word comprised my intolerable duty — 'Depart!' (he begs her to accept his pledge of fidelity)

'I will keep the law given by God; sanctioned by man. I will hold to the principles received by me when I was sane, and not mad — as I am now' (Jane is determined)

...mentally, I still possessed my soul, and with it the certainty of ultimate safety (as above)

'My daughter, flee temptation!' (the moon metamorphoses into human form)

'Mother, I will' (Jane listens to her mentor's advice)

Gentle reader...never may you, like me, dread to be the instrument of evil to what you wholly love (Jane feels guilt at abandoning Mr Rochester)

## Chapter XXVIII

I have no relative but the universal mother, Nature (Jane, alone on the moors)

We know that God is everywhere; but certainly we feel His presence most when His works are on the grandest scale spread before us; and it is in the unclouded night-sky, where His worlds wheel their silent course, that we read clearest His infinitude, His omnipotence, His omnipresence (as above)

The burden must be carried; the want provided for; the suffering endured; the responsibility fulfilled. I set out (as above)

## Chapter XXIX

Prejudices, it is well known, are most difficult to eradicate from the heart whose soil has never been loosened or fertilised by education (Jane criticises Hannah)

Had he been a statue instead of a man, he could not have been easier (St John)

'I owe to their spontaneous, genuine, genial compassion as large a debt as to your evangelical charity' (Jane speaks to St John of his sisters)

## Chapter XXX

...pleasure arising from perfect congeniality of tastes, sentiments, and principles (Jane feels that Diana and Mary are kindred spirits)

I was sure St John Rivers — pure-lived, conscientious, zealous as he was — had not yet found that peace of God which passeth all understanding (Jane recognises St John's restlessness)

It was plodding — but then, compared with that of a governess in a rich house, it was independent; and the fear of servitude with strangers entered my soul like iron (Jane speaking of her teaching position)

'...human affections and sympathies have a most powerful hold on you' (St John to Jane)

## Chapter XXXI

I felt — yes, idiot that I am — I felt degraded (because her pupils are working class)

'It is hard work to control the workings of inclination and turn the bent of nature' (St John speaking of himself)

'...the heart of a politician, of a soldier, of a votary of glory, a lover of renown, a luster after power, beat under my curate's surplice' (as above)

## Chapter XXXII

'Solitude is at least as bad for you as it is for me' (Jane to St John)

He had not imagined that a woman would dare to speak so to a man (St John referring to Jane)

'Reason, and not feeling, is my guide' (St John)

## Chapter XXXIII

'And then,' he pursued, 'I am cold: no fervour infects me' (St John)

'Whereas I am hot, and fire dissolves ice' (Jane)

Glorious discovery to a lonely wretch! This was wealth indeed! — wealth to the heart! — a mine of pure, genial affections (Jane learns that the Rivers are her cousins)

'And you...cannot imagine the craving I have for fraternal and sisterly love. I never had a home' (as above)

## Chapter XXXIV

Literally, he lived only to aspire — after what was good and great, certainly; but still he would never rest (Jane observes St John)

...he was of the material from which nature hews her heroes (as above)

I fell under a freezing spell. When he said 'go', I went; 'come', I came; 'do this', I did it. But I did not love my servitude (Jane of her relationship with St John)

I daily wished more to please him: but to do so, I felt daily more and more that I must disown half my nature (as above)

I never in my life have known any medium in my dealings with positive, hard characters, antagonistic to my own, between absolute submission and determined revolt (Jane about herself)

The glen and sky spun round: the hills heaved! It was as if I had heard a summons from Heaven (Jane is tempted to go to India with St John)

...is not the occupation he now offers me truly the most glorious man can adopt or God assign? Is it not, by its noble cares and sublime results, the one best calculated to fill the void left by uptorn affections and demolished hopes? (as above)

If I join St John, I abandon half myself (she hesitates)

...attached to him only in this capacity: my body would be under rather a stringent yoke, but my heart and mind would be free (she agrees to go as his adopted sister)

## Chapter XXXV

Had I attended to the suggestions of pride and ire, I should immediately have left him (Jane is angry at St John's coolness towards her)

'He is a good and a great man; but he forgets, pitilessly, the feelings and claims of little people, in pursuing his own large views' (Jane to Diana about St John)

To have yielded then would have been an error of principle: to have yielded now would have been an error of judgment (Jane about standing up to Mr Rochester and St John)

I sincerely, deeply, fervently longed to do what was right; and only that. 'Show me, show me the path!' I entreated of Heaven (Jane asks whether it is God's will that she marry St John)

It was *my* time to assume ascendancy. *My* powers were in play, and in force (Jane has heard Mr Rochester's voice)

## Chapter XXXVI

The wondrous shock of feeling had...opened the door of the soul's cell, and loosed its bands (Jane recalls hearing the voice)

## Chapter XXXVII

But in his countenance I saw a change: that looked desperate and brooding — that reminded me of some wronged and fettered wild beast or bird, dangerous to approach in his sullen woe. The caged eagle, whose gold-ringed eyes cruelty has extinguished, might look as looked that sightless Samson (Jane of Mr Rochester at Ferndean)

…with him I was at perfect ease, because I knew I suited him. Delightful consciousness!…in his presence I thoroughly lived; and he lived in mine (as above)

'I love you better now, when I can really be useful to you' (Jane to Mr Rochester)

'Of late…I began to see and acknowledge the hand of God in my doom. I began to experience remorse, repentance, the wish for reconcilement to my Maker' (Mr Rochester)

'I humbly entreat my Redeemer to give me strength to lead henceforth a purer life than I have done hitherto!' (as above)

## Chapter XXXVIII

I hold myself supremely blest — blest beyond what language can express (Jane in the novel's present, ten years after they married)

I am: ever more absolutely bone of his bone and flesh of his flesh (Jane of her husband)

…his glorious sun hastens to its setting (Jane of St John)

# Literary terms and concepts

The terms and concepts below have been selected for their relevance to talking and writing about *Jane Eyre*. It will aid argument and expression to become familiar with them and to use them in your essays, provided that you can support them with examples from the text and explain their effect.

| | |
|---|---|
| **allegory** | extended metaphor that veils a moral or political underlying meaning |
| **alliteration** | repetition of initial letter or sound in adjacent words to create an atmospheric or onomatopoeic effect, e.g. 'haughty Hate', 'furious frown' (p. 314) |
| **allusion** | passing reference to another literary work, without naming it |
| **analogy** | perception of similarity between two things |
| **antagonist** | a person who opposes the hero or protagonist |
| **antithesis** | contrasting of ideas by balancing words or phrases of opposite meaning, e.g. 'Breakfast was over, and none had breakfasted' (p. 55) |

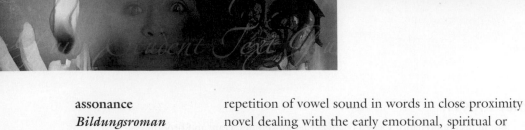

| | |
|---|---|
| assonance | repetition of vowel sound in words in close proximity |
| *Bildungsroman* | novel dealing with the early emotional, spiritual or educational development of its hero/heroine |
| caricature | exaggerated and ridiculous portrayal of a person built around a specific physical or personality trait |
| characterisation | means by which fictional characters are personified and made distinctive |
| climax | moment of intensity to which a series of events has been leading |
| closure | sense of an ending; tying up the loose ends in a fictional work |
| colloquial | informal language of conversational speech |
| connotations | associations evoked by a word, e.g. 'flat' suggests dull and uninteresting |
| contextuality | historical, social and cultural background of a text |
| dénouement | unfolding of the final stages of a plot, when all is revealed |
| *deus ex machina* | literally, the god from the machine; a supernatural intervention that resolves a difficult situation or furthers the action |
| dialogue | direct speech of characters engaged in conversation |
| diction | choice of words; vocabulary from a particular semantic field, e.g. religion |
| didactic | with the intention of teaching the reader and instilling moral values |
| dramatic irony | when the audience knows something the character speaking does not, which creates humour or tension |
| empathy | identifying with a character in a literary work |
| epiphany | sudden and striking revelation of the essence of something sublime |
| eponymous | main character after whom a work is named, e.g. *Jane Eyre* |
| eulogy | speech or writing in praise of someone or something |
| figurative | using imagery; non-literal use of language |
| foreshadowing | arranging events and information so that later events are prepared for |
| genre | type or form of writing with identifiable characteristics |
| Gothic | medieval genre, revived in late eighteenth century, which contains violence, death, horror, the supernatural and the macabre; set in eerie ancient buildings, such as castles, during darkness and bad weather |

| | |
|---|---|
| **imagery** | descriptive language appealing to the senses; imagery may be sustained or recurring throughout texts, usually in the form of **simile** or **metaphor** |
| **irony** | language intended to mean the opposite of the words expressed; or amusing or cruel reversal of an outcome expected, intended or deserved; situation in which one is mocked by fate or the facts |
| **juxtaposition** | placing side by side for (ironic) contrast of interpretation |
| **metaphor** | suppressed comparison implied not stated, e.g. 'the instrument of evil' (p. 370) |
| **motif** | recurring verbal or structural device that reminds the audience of a theme |
| **myth** | fiction involving supernatural beings that explains natural and social phenomena and embodies traditional and popular ideas |
| **narrative** | connected and usually chronological series of events to form a story |
| **pathetic fallacy** | attributing emotions to inanimate objects, usually elements of nature, to represent the persona's feelings, e.g. describing the sky as melancholy |
| **pathos** | evocation of pity by a situation of suffering and helplessness |
| **peripeteia** | sudden reversal of fortune for a literary character |
| **personification** | human embodiment of an abstraction or object, using capital letter or he/she |
| **plosive** | a stop consonant released quickly (p, b, t, d, k, g) |
| **plot** | cause-and-effect sequence of events caused by characters' actions |
| **poetic justice** | appropriate and often ironic rewarding of virtue and punishment of evil |
| **protagonist** | the principal character |
| **realism and idealism** | associated with the rise of the novel in the early eighteenth century, realism refers to the depiction of detailed, accurately observed scenery, objects, characters and behaviours; it contrasts with idealism, which filters out unpalatable realities and individual experience or perception |
| **reflective** | revealing thoughts of writer or character |
| **register** | type of expression, level of formality |
| **Romanticism** | influential artistic movement of the late-eighteenth and early-nineteenth centuries, characterised by the |

|  |  |
|---|---|
|  | rebellious assertion of the individual and a belief in the spiritual correspondence between humankind and nature |
| **satire** | exposing of vice or foolishness of a person or institution to ridicule ; a *Guardian* editorial defined satire as 'comedy taken to a pitch where it could force change through a stinging mix of popularity, derision and shame' (10 October 2007) |
| **semantic field** | group of words with thematic relationship, e.g. cross, candle, gold |
| **semantics** | study of influence of words on thought and behaviour |
| **simile** | comparison introduced by 'as' or 'like' |
| **stereotype** | a category of person with typical characteristics, often used for mockery |
| **style** | selection and organisation of language elements, related to genre or individual user of language |
| **subtext** | the layer of meaning that lies below the surface of a text; what is not actually said or done but may be deduced by the reader |
| **symbol** | object, person or event that represents something more than itself |
| **synopsis** | summary of plot |
| **syntax** | arrangement of grammar and word order in sentence construction |
| **theme** | abstract idea or issue explored in a text |
| **tone** | emotional aspect of the voice of a text |

# Questions & Answers

# LITERATURE

# Essay questions, specimen plans and notes

## Coursework titles

There are different styles of coursework title depending on which board you are studying for. Your teacher will guide you to an appropriate format, but here are some suggestions.

### Creative (personal/original writing) interpretation

1 How does Brontë's way of structuring *Jane Eyre* affect your interpretation of the novel?

2 How does Brontë's use of imagery and symbolism affect your interpretation of the novel?

3 How does Brontë's use of first-person narrative affect your interpretation of the novel?

### Creative/transformational writing

1 Write Diana Rivers's account of Jane's story creating Diana's voice, capturing Brontë's style and tone and building on Brontë's realisation of character.

2 Write Mr Mason's account of his experiences, creating Mr Mason's voice, capturing Brontë's style and tone and building on Brontë's realisation of the character.

3 Write Mr Rochester's account of the ten years of his marriage to Jane, creating Mr Rochester's voice, capturing Brontë's style and tone and building on Brontë's realisation of character.

4 Write Bertha's thoughts as she sits alone in her attic, shortly before she sets fire to Thornfield Hall, creating Bertha's voice, capturing Brontë's style and tone and building on Brontë's realisation of character.

### Prose study

1 'For a large part of the nineteenth century, the English novel was significantly limited by the necessity to conform to a moral code which aimed to protect a predominantly female readership from exposure to sexual corruption.' Basing your response on a comparison of *Jane Eyre* and one other novel by Charlotte Brontë, discuss to what extent you agree with this view.

2 'Considering the time in which she wrote, Charlotte Brontë's female characters are surprisingly outspoken.' Basing your response on a comparison of *Jane Eyre* and one other novel by Charlotte Brontë, discuss to what extent you agree with this view.

3 'The poetic intensity of [Charlotte Brontë's] writing, together with the patent influences of the Gothic and Byronic traditions, make [her] works most striking inheritors of Romanticism in the fiction of the period.' Basing your response on

a comparison of *Jane Eyre* and one other novel by Charlotte Brontë, discuss to what extent you agree with this view.

**4** Basing your response on a comparison of *Jane Eyre* and *Wide Sargasso Sea*, explore the importance of place in two novels written more than 100 years apart.

**5** A comparative study of the presentation of contemporary perceptions of madness in *Jane Eyre* and *Wide Sargasso Sea*.

**6** Basing your response on a comparison of *Jane Eyre* and *Wide Sargasso Sea*, explore how Charlotte Brontë and Jean Rhys, writing more than 100 years apart, tackle feminist issues.

### Creative reading

This format offers you the opportunity to write creatively in a chosen literary genre in response to your wider reading of a prose text and to write a commentary on your creative response. You are free to write in any genre, but the stimulus for writing must be a prose text, other than those prose texts selected for the prose study.

## Exam essays

The suggested essay questions that follow can be used for planning practice and/or full essay writing, for classroom timed practice or for homework. They are based on the various styles of question set by the different boards. It is important to check which Assessment Objectives you need to cover, as the boards have different requirements. You will find some essay titles with suggestions for ideas to include in a plan, and there are two with guidance from the board on how to approach the question. Sample student answers are provided for two of the questions.

### Passage-based questions

Examiners advise that reference to the rest of the text should form as much as 60% of the essay, even for a passage-based question. Focus closely on the passage, but also relate its content and/or language to elsewhere in the text and to the partner text, if there is one. Make connections both backwards and forwards, and link your comments to the overall themes and/or structure of the novels. Start by placing the passage in its context and summarising the situation. Include references to character, event, theme and language, and ask yourself how the episode modifies or adds to our understanding so far, and how typical it is of the novel as a whole. Think about reader reaction, using your own as the basis for your analysis.

Here are the questions to address when analysing a passage from this novel:

- Why has Brontë included this passage in the novel? What is its importance?
- How does this passage fit into the narrative structure of the novel?
- Which of the themes is Brontë evoking here, and how does this passage fit into her treatment of that theme in the whole novel?
- What previous scenes do we need to recall in order to understand fully the implications of this passage?

- Does this extract foreshadow any future scenes?
- It is a first-person narrative, so how reliable is Jane's account at this point?
- What Jane is thinking as she writes may be different from what she says to her nineteenth-century readers, so what is the subtext here?
- Can you identify the voice of the mature Jane Rochester, or is she reconstructing events as she remembers them?
- What does this passage reveal about Jane: her character, her feelings, her thoughts?
- Until the final chapter, Jane withholds the information that she did marry Mr Rochester. Is she withholding anything else at this point?
- Does Brontë use any recurring images or symbols in this passage? If so, analyse how they fit into the overall pattern.
- If there is some description, what mood is Brontë evoking and how does she do it?
- Is there any speech in this passage? If so, what does it add to the effectiveness, and what does it tell us about the speaker?
- Are there any particular words or metaphors that would reward close analysis?
- Is this one of the times when Brontë uses the present tense to give a sense of immediacy and involve the reader in Jane's thoughts?
- What comparisons and/or contrasts can you make with your partner text?

## Specimen question

'**Relatives should be respected and loved, yet in Literature they are often cruel and evil.**'

Using *Jane Eyre* p. 19 as your starting point, from '**I was a discord in Gateshead Hall;**' to '**and to see an uncongenial alien permanently intruded on her own family group.**' p. 20, explore the presentation of relatives.

**In your response, you should focus on *Jane Eyre* to establish your argument and you should refer to the second text you have read to support and develop your line of argument.**

### Advice from the board of examiners

Responses are likely to include reference to the following in establishing an argument using *Jane Eyre*:

- their interpretation of the way Jane's aunt is presented
- this interpretation to be based on the way she speaks and acts towards Jane
- an analysis of the language used to present alienation
- the way that Brontë has invited the reader to pass judgement on the cruel and evil nature of Jane's relatives

### Possible ideas to include in a plan

- The first thing you should do is to explain what you understand by the terms in the question: 'cruel' and 'evil'. These are subjective terms, so try to empathise with Mrs Reed.

From her point of view, it would not have been cruel to put Jane into a comfortably furnished room to calm down. It turned out to be cruel only because of Jane's vivid imagination. She is a God-fearing woman, trying to bring Jane up as befits her station as a poor relation. As mid-nineteenth century society required, she is trying to instil 'perfect submission and stillness'. Mrs Reed can be perceived as resentful and afraid rather than evil, and not 'cruel' but a product of her society and its prejudices.

- This leads neatly into a consideration of Brontë's narrative technique. Jane is a biased narrator, who wants her readers to understand why she was unhappy and so focuses on her feelings at the time. However, Brontë also wants to show that the mature Jane has a deeper understanding of past events.

- As you provide evidence of these points, you could explore the use of past and present tenses, the semantics of 'thing', the role of the weather in influencing Jane's mood, and Brontë's use of questions.

- It is advisable to spend about a third of your essay on your analysis of the passage. Another third should be spent widening your exploration of the theme/characters through the whole book. It is significant that the board does not seem to expect an analysis of Jane's other relatives. However, references to the Rivers family will help to establish a good line of argument. For instance, you may argue that, while Jane has one set of relatives who reject her, Brontë balances the theme by providing another set who take her into their family circle.

- The final third of your essay should concentrate on supporting and developing your line of argument by comparing and contrasting *Jane Eyre* with your second text. If you have read *Wide Sargasso Sea*, for instance, you could compare Mrs Reed's weakness in complying with her dead husband's wishes but letting her resentment affect her attitude to the child with Richard Mason's weak reply to his sister's plea for help: 'I cannot interfere legally between yourself and your husband.'

- You could compare Mrs Reed's resentment with Daniel Cosway's resentment that he has nothing whereas his half-sister is a substantial heiress. Mrs Reed tries to prevent Jane from becoming an heiress by lying in response to Jane's uncle's letter; Daniel ruins Antoinette's happiness.

- You could show that Rhys also balances resentful relatives with a kind one in Sandi Cosway.

- You could draw parallels between Antoinette and Jane. Jane's aunt pushes her away and sends her to school; Antoinette's mother pushes her away in favour of her sick son, Pierre, 'as if she had decided for once and for all that I was useless to her'.

## Further questions

**1** '**Jane Eyre is very responsive to the atmosphere of the places where she lives.**'
Using *Jane Eyre* **p. 16 as your starting point, from 'The red-room was a spare chamber,' to 'a sense of dreary consecration had guarded it from frequent intrusion.' p. 17, explore the presentation of indoor settings.**

In your response, you should focus on *Jane Eyre* to establish your argument and you should refer to the second text you have read to support and develop your line of argument.

*Notes*

- When you are asked to explore 'presentation', you should focus on the language Brontë has chosen, explaining her narrative technique and looking closely at tenses, metaphors, connotation, association etc. and how they reveal Jane's feelings.
- Spend about a third of your essay analysing Brontë's description of Jane's response to being locked in the red-room.
- In the middle part of your essay, select two or three other settings to explore in detail. The third storey of Thornfield Hall offers a couple of excellent passages in Chapter XI when Jane is being shown round and compares the corridor with Bluebeard's castle and in Chapter XX when she is tending Mr Mason and the faces on the apostle cabinet seem to come alive in the flickering candlelight.
- You should also look closely at Jane as a self-conscious narrator and explore her relationship with her readers.
- Finally, you must explore connections and comparisons with your chosen partner text.

**2** 'Ms Eyre is very responsive to nature and its moods.'

Using *Jane Eyre* p. 286 as your starting point, from 'A splendid Midsummer shone over England:' to 'my step is stayed — not by sound, not by sight, but once more by a warning fragrance.' p. 287, explore the presentation of natural surroundings.

In your response, you should focus on *Jane Eyre* to establish your argument and you should refer to the second text you have read to support and develop your line of argument.

**3** 'Symbolism is a very effective tool for a novelist.'

Using *Jane Eyre* p. 367 as your starting point, from 'That night I never thought to sleep;' to '"Mother, I will."' p. 367, explore the use of symbols.

In your response, you should focus on *Jane Eyre* to establish your argument and you should refer to the second text you have read to support and develop your line of argument.

**4** 'It is true to say that class always divides and it never unites.'

Using *Jane Eyre* p. 205 as your starting point, from 'Mrs Dent here bent over to the pious lady,' to '"My lily-flower, you are right now, as always."' p. 206, explore the portrayal of class and its role in the novel.

In your response, you should focus on *Jane Eyre* to establish your argument and you should refer to the second text you have read to support and develop your line of argument.

## Whole-text questions — open text

**Specimen question**

*Jane Eyre* (Penguin Classics) and either *Wide Sargasso Sea* (Penguin Modern Classics) or *The Magic Toyshop* (Virago)

**'Ms Eyre is one of those heroines who refuses to blend into the traditional female position of subservience and who stands up for her beliefs.'**

**Explore how the female position is presented.**

**In your response, you should focus on *Jane Eyre* to establish your argument and you should refer to the second text you have read to support and develop your line of argument.**

### *Advice from the board of examiners*

Responses are likely to include reference to the following:

- their interpretation of the way Jane is presented
- Jane's nature: in particular her perceived stubbornness
- how she relates to other characters in the context of the traditional female role
- possible readings and interpretations of the notion of a heroine
- Jane's own beliefs and how she stands by them
- an analysis of the notion of 'subservience'
- a comparison between Jane and other female characters in a way that will bring out readers' interpretations of them
- an exploration of language, imagery and description

**Further questions**

**1** **'Ms Eyre is one of those heroines who demands equality with her social superiors.'**
**Explore how social class is presented.**

**In your response, you should focus on *Jane Eyre* to establish your argument and you should refer to the second text you have read to support and develop your line of argument.**

### *Notes*

- Use the quotation as a starting point, offering evidence of Jane's strong convictions; you could quote from Chapters XVII and XVIII, perhaps, and her dramatic declaration in Chapter XXIII.
- As always, you must explain Brontë's narrative technique and show evidence of Jane's convictions. For instance, she believes that her working class pupils are 'as good as the scions of gentlest genealogy'.
- Then you should move on to a detailed consideration of the ways in which Brontë presents class differences at this period of history when the Industrial Revolution was upsetting the status quo. You could explore the position of governesses, the way in which Mr Rochester's house guests are presented, the presentation of servants and Rosamond Oliver's social rise.
- For AO3 you must explore connections and comparisons with your chosen partner text.

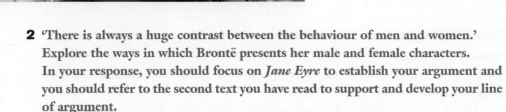

**2** 'There is always a huge contrast between the behaviour of men and women.'
Explore the ways in which Brontë presents her male and female characters.
In your response, you should focus on *Jane Eyre* to establish your argument and you should refer to the second text you have read to support and develop your line of argument.

**3** 'In Literature, a first-person narrator is always unreliable.'
Explore how the narrative technique affects audience response.
In your response, you should focus on *Jane Eyre* to establish your argument and you should refer to the second text you have read to support and develop your line of argument.

**4** 'Female characters are often represented as being constrained by their societies.'
Explore the presentation of female characters in the light of this statement.
In your response, you should focus on *Jane Eyre* to establish your argument and you should refer to the second text you have read to support and develop your line of argument.

### Whole-text questions — closed text

**1** 'Jane Rochester brings a mature balance to her narrative.'
How far and in what ways do you agree with this comment on the narrative method of *Jane Eyre*?

*Possible ideas to include in a plan*

- If the board asks 'How far do you agree?' you are expected to agree to a certain extent and then disagree. For this question you need to analyse Brontë's use of a retrospective narrator and how the novel is structured. An overview of the narrative technique makes a good introduction to your essay, and this leads satisfyingly in to close detailed analysis of characterisation and language in the middle of your essay.

- You could argue that, at Gateshead and Lowood, the mature narrator helps the reader to understand feelings and thoughts that the child cannot articulate. However, once she falls in love with Mr Rochester, her narrative becomes unreliable as she wishes to present him positively, and she is trying to withhold the information that she eventually marries him.

- An alternative line of argument might be that she does offer a mature balance in assessing her feelings and motives as a child and a young woman, but her language choices reveal that she still feels strong emotions, and Brontë's own prejudices sometimes seem to intrude.

- As evidence you could demonstrate how Brontë's experiences as governess have coloured Jane's attitude to children, both Adèle and her pupils at Morton, as well as to middle-class mothers. In Chapter XII, she comments on the cool language with which she describes Adèle, explaining 'I am not writing to flatter parental egotism, to echo cant, or prop up humbug; I am merely telling the truth.' This apparently balanced judgement reveals deep prejudice against the Victorian's idealisation of middle- and upper-class children in her use of strong colloquial language and harsh plosive consonants.

- At the end of Chapter XXVII, Jane Rochester's language makes clear that, even at the time of writing, she still feels guilty for doing the right thing and leaving him. Mr Rochester has made her feel that she was 'the instrument of evil', an emotionally charged metaphor. It is a good idea to try to write in analytical sentences to make sure you offer your evidence (the quotation), a literary term to define or describe the feature to which you wish to draw attention, an explanation of why Brontë has used it, as well as an evaluation of what has been achieved.
- Occasionally, Brontë makes Jane Rochester use the present and future tenses, as in Chapter XXXI when she writes of feeling degraded by becoming a village schoolteacher. Usually, however, Brontë uses the past tense, even when she implies immediacy with the adverb 'now' as in Chapter XXXV when Jane is comparing her resistance to St John with her resistance to Mr Rochester: 'To have yielded then would have been an error of principle; to have yielded now would have been an error of judgment.'
- In the last third of your essay you should make insightful comparisons with additional appropriate texts, such as other nineteenth-century novels, or other fictional autobiographies.
- For AO4, you need to offer informed insight into the importance of such contextual issues as nineteenth-century attitudes to gender roles and social class, as well as Brontë's own experiences and views.

(Note: see Sample essay 1 below for a student response to this question.)

### Further questions

**2** 'The settings of *Jane Eyre* represent stages in the development of Jane's character.'
How far and in what ways do you find this to be the case?

**3** 'Symbolism is central to the meaning and effects of *Jane Eyre*.'
In the light of this comment, consider ways in which symbolism is used in *Jane Eyre*.

**4** 'Because *Jane Eyre* is a first-person narrative, none of the characters other than Jane is fully developed.'
How far and in what ways do you agree with this view?

**5** '*Jane Eyre* is little more than an unrealistic romance in which the Cinderella heroine succeeds in marrying her prince.'
How far and in what ways do you agree with this view?

**6** 'Ms Eyre has a very strong religious faith which helps her choose the right path in moments of crisis.'
How far and in what ways do you find this to be the case?
(Note: see Sample essay 2 for a student response to this question.)

**7** '*Jane Eyre* proves that Charlotte Brontë is a true Romantic writer.'
In the light of this comment, consider the ways in which Brontë can be called a Romantic writer.

**8** '*Jane Eyre* is a feminist heroine who demands equality for women.'
How far and in what ways do you agree with this statement?

# Sample essays

## Sample essay 1

**'Jane Rochester brings a mature balance to her narrative.'**
**How far and in what ways do you agree with this comment on the narrative method of *Jane Eyre*?**

Charlotte Brontë chose for Jane to write her supposed autobiography when she has been happily married for ten years. As Jane supposedly writes about her growing up, she seems to be trying to understand her own behaviour as well as that of others. The conventional Victorian attitude to the poor was that they should be grateful for the generosity of their benefactors, however grudging, but Jane recalls her angry and resentful thoughts and feelings at the time. However, she sometimes adds more measured comments from an adult perspective. At Gateshead, for instance, she notes that 'children can feel but they cannot analyse their feelings'. Attempting to balance passion with reason, she asks 'how could [her aunt] really like an interloper?' and seems to accept that 'It must have been most irksome'.

Similarly, as a child, she describes herself as unable to answer 'the ceaseless inward question — why I thus suffered', but the adult says that, at a distance, she can see it clearly. However, although she may understand her aunt and cousins, the language Brontë gives her reveals that she has not achieved a 'mature balance', as the rage she felt as a child at being treated like a 'thing' is still there. Each time she repeats this non-human epithet, the premodifying adjective is stronger and reveals more pain, until the fourth time she refers to herself in her aunt's eyes as 'a noxious thing', as if she is actually harmful. As she mentally addresses her aunt, Jane Rochester actually admits, in the present tense: 'I ought to forgive you', but clearly she has not yet done so.

As she narrates events at Lowood, Jane Rochester is able to balance anger with understanding as she sympathises with the teachers, 'poor things'. She comments philosophically on Miss Scatcherd's bullying of the saintly Helen, using a cosmic metaphor: 'Such is the imperfect nature of man! Such spots are there on the disc of the clearest planet; and eyes like Miss Scatcherd's can only see those minute defects, and are blind to the full brightness of the orb.' Instead of presenting herself as perfect, Jane humbly admits 'I am a defective being, with many faults and few redeeming points'. However, Brontë suggests that she does not feel as humble as she thinks she should be. She frequently passes judgement on those less intelligent than her and, when she takes the job of village schoolmistress at Morton, she 'felt degraded'; she feared she 'had taken a step which sank instead of raising me in the scale of social existence'. Jane has absorbed the social prejudices of the nineteenth-century society in which she lives. Nevertheless, Brontë shows that Jane Rochester is aware that she should not have these snobbish feelings, and, in the future tense, she writes 'I shall strive to overcome them'. So, although Jane has not yet managed to balance reason with feeling, she is working towards it as she writes.

However, Jane does not always seem aware that her narrative lacks the rational balance she leads us to expect. When Eliza declares her intention to enter a nunnery, without any awareness of her religious prejudice against Roman Catholicism, Jane remembers thinking 'much good may it do you'. This may well reflect Brontë's own prejudice, as her father was a clergyman in the evangelical wing of the Anglican church. Jane's bias in favour of Mr Rochester is also clearly evident as she always excuses his behaviour or presents him favourably. For instance, she observes that, when he was wrestling with Bertha, 'he would not strike her'. For a twenty-first century reader, there is no mature balance to be found in admiration for a man because he does not strike a woman, however mad, although, in the nineteenth century, people considered mad were often subjected to violent treatment.

Jane is a self-conscious narrator, frequently withholding information from her readers in order to create suspense. However, sometimes, when she does this, it can make her sound naïve or melodramatic rather than balanced. Her exaggerated surprise that Mr Rochester is aware of her presence in the orchard, asking 'could his shadow feel?', rings hollow because the reader has guessed that he followed her. When invited by St John to go for a walk, she prefaces the incident with observations about her character, and how she gives 'absolute submission' until she bursts 'with volcanic vehemence' into 'determined revolt'. This apparently hyperbolic metaphor raises our anticipation that this is going to be no ordinary walk, and the use of the present tense reveals that she still has difficulty controlling her passion when pushed too far.

Eventually, in the final chapter, all is revealed and all the loose ends tied up. However, the reader might doubt that Jane has achieved the mature balance she has been striving for. Her declarations of love for her husband, such as 'I know no weariness of my Edward's society', 'we are ever together', 'We talk, I believe, all day long', are made in absolutes which may prompt us to ask when she has found time to write her autobiography. She feels the need to tell us three times 'Never did I weary' of supporting him when he was totally blind, so we might ask whether she is trying to persuade herself, especially when she merely 'bestows' her confidence on him while his is 'devoted' to her, and when he loves her 'truly' while she only loves him 'fondly'.

Brontë has used her adult narrator to bring a mature balance to this story of a girl growing to womanhood, but she has also managed to show that Jane Rochester has not yet achieved the equilibrium between reason and emotion she seeks. The final page of the novel leaves us with the impression that part of her wishes that she had gone to India with St John to exercise her faculties in the occupation which, at the time of the British Empire, was considered 'the most glorious man can adopt

or God assign'. As she told us before Mr Rochester arrived at Thornfield: 'Women feel just as men feel; they need exercise for their faculties and a field for their efforts as much as their brothers do'.

## Sample essay 2

**'Jane Eyre has a very strong religious faith which helps her to choose the right path in moments of crisis.'**
**How far and in what ways do you find this to be the case?**

Through Jane Rochester's fictional autobiography, Brontë explores the development of Jane's religious faith, starting with her acknowledgement that naughty children go to hell and burn in a pit full of fire. Even then, however, she is thinking for herself, and she brings her own unorthodox childish logic to the question of how to avoid this fate: 'I must keep in good health and not die'. In the nineteenth century, life expectancy was low, so people were very preoccupied with what happened after death. The church exploited their fear, threatening damnation to those who did not conform and salvation to the submissive.

At Lowood she is presented with two extremes. The inflexible Mr Brocklehurst believes Jane is already 'a castaway', a soul predestined for damnation, according to his Calvinist doctrine; her body must be punished in an attempt to save her soul, 'if indeed such salvation be possible'. By contrast, Helen Burns believes God 'will never destroy what he created', and she is certain that there is 'a region of happiness' where we will all be received after death by our 'mighty universal Parent'. At this time, however, Jane doubts 'that there is such a place as heaven; and that our souls can get to it when we die'. So Brontë shows Jane as a child listening to others but thinking for herself.

As an adult, Jane does not talk about religion, but it clearly underpins her life. In discussions with Mr Rochester, she reveals a strong faith, warning him that 'the human and fallible should not arrogate a power with which the divine and perfect alone can be safely entrusted'. Jane quotes from the Bible frequently but naturally, without drawing attention to this, as when, quoting from the Psalms, she describes the schoolroom as 'a very pleasant refuge in time of trouble'. Brontë often gives her language with religious associations, such as when she rescues Mr Rochester from the fire and 'baptised the couch afresh', and, 'by God's aid, succeeded in extinguishing the flames'. In a moment of crisis, she feels that God supports her.

Nevertheless, when she has to make decisions, she turns not to God but to a strong moral sense and her own self-respect. She tells Rochester: 'I like to serve you, sir, and to obey you in all that is right.' Her advice to him, when he confides that he seeks reformation, is that 'Men and women die; philosophers falter in wisdom, and Christians in goodness: if anyone you know has suffered and erred, let him look higher than his equals for strength to amend and solace to heal'. Brontë suggests that Jane feels that we cannot rely on anybody else for guidance, so it is to our consciences we must turn to learn God's will. This is perhaps surprising for a writer whose father was a clergyman.

In supposedly looking back over her life, Brontë shows that Jane is aware that her love for Rochester 'stood between me and every thought of religion...I could not, in those days, see God for His creature, of whom I had made an idol'. Rochester recognises this when she is terrified by her night-time visitor and turns to him rather than God. He can see that when she says she loves him she speaks with 'earnest religious energy' and gazes at him with 'the very sublime of faith, truth and devotion'. When her idol is revealed as a flawed sinner at the altar, she is totally bereft: 'One idea only still throbbed life-like within me — a remembrance of God.'

In extremis, then, it is to her religion she turns, but it is the moon, meta-morphosed into human form in a dream, who tells her to flee temptation. It is her strong moral sense and belief in God that guide her as she leaves Thornfield: 'God must have led me on', but the modal auxiliary shows that she lacks the certainty of Helen Burns. At Whitcross, it is to 'the universal mother, Nature' she turns for comfort, like a true Romantic. Only later, after her meal, does she say her evening prayers, as if by routine. Sleeping under the stars, however, she feels the presence of God and 'His infinitude, His omnipotence, His omnipresence'. Nature and God are not separate influences: for Jane, to love nature is to love God.

At last, she becomes convinced by Helen's belief in the evangelical doctrine of individual regeneration, that 'neither earth should perish, nor one of the souls it treasured'. Reassured that God will guard Mr Rochester, she sleeps well. Next day, after struggling to fend for herself, Jane sinks onto the doorstep at Moor House, saying: 'I can but die...I believe in God. Let me try to wait His will in silence.' Brontë shows her readers that, when Jane finally gives herself totally into God's hands, God sends a rescuer in the form of St John Rivers.

The next crisis in her life is when St John proposes to her. She is tempted by missionary work, which seems to her 'the most glorious man can adopt or God assign', but she refuses to sacrifice her 'unblighted self' to a man who does not love her. The third time he asks, she is tempted to resign her sense of self: 'Religion called — Angels beckoned — God commanded.' She entreats heaven to show her the path, and that is when she hears Mr Rochester's voice. However, she ascribes this strange phenomenon not to God but to nature. Brontë suggests that this moment of epiphany reveals to Jane that the self is important as well as God: 'It was *my* time to assume ascendancy. *My* powers were in play, and in force.'

What sends her back to Rochester is a conviction that she belongs with him and that it is natural for them to be together — a conviction that nature is a manifestation of God. Jane has found a balance between religious conviction, represented by St John, and natural inclination, represented by Mr Rochester. Luckily the latter has turned to God and his first wife is dead, so she is able to end her story without compromising either her religious faith or her natural inclination. Because Jane's religious faith is an integral part of her, her conscience and her integrity guide her to choose the right path in moments of crisis.

# Further study

## Biographies

Barker, J. (1994) *The Brontës*, Weidenfeld and Nicolson
Barker, J. (ed.) (1998) *The Brontës: A Life in Letters*, Overlook Press
Gaskell, E. (1857) *The Life of Charlotte Brontë*, Dent and Sons

## Criticism

Allott, M. (ed.) (1973) *Charlotte Brontë: Jane Eyre and Villette*, Macmillan Casebook Series
Beer, P. (1974) *Reader, I Married Him*, Macmillan Papermac
Davies, S. (ed.) (2006) *Jane Eyre*, Penguin Classics
Eagleton, T. (1975) *Myths of Power: A Marxist Study of the Brontës*, The Macmillan Press
Gilbert, S. M. and Gubar, S. (1979) *The Madwoman in the Attic*, Yale University Press
Gordon, F. (1989) *A Preface to the Brontës*, Longman
Newman, B. (ed.) (1996) *Jane Eyre: Charlotte Brontë*, Bedford/St Martin's
Sherry, N. (1969) *Charlotte and Emily Brontë*, Evans, Literature in Perspective
Showalter, E. (1999) *A Literature of Their Own: British Women Novelists from Brontë to Lessing*, Virago
Winnifrith, T. and Chitham, E. (1989) *Charlotte and Emily Brontë*, Macmillan Literary Lives

## Magazine articles

Byrne, S. (November 2000) 'Women writing, women talking', *The English Review*
Frost, R. (November 1999) 'The fable of the poor orphan child', *The English Review*
Havely, C. P. (September 2005) 'The Eyre affair', *The English Review*
Havely, C. P. (November 2006) 'Troubles with men', *The English Review*
Head, K. (April 1995) '*Wide Sargasso Sea*: a devil of a book', *The English Review*
Wood, M. (February 2006) 'Jane Eyre in the red-room', *The English Review*

# Films

1944: directed by Robert Stevenson, starring Joan Fontaine and Orson Welles

1970: directed by Delbert Mann, starring Susannah York and George C. Scott

1975: directed by Joan Craft, starring Sorcha Cusack and Michael Jayston (BBC)

1983: directed by Julian Aymes, starring Zelah Clarke and Timothy Dalton (BBC)

1996: directed by Franco Zeffirelli, starring Charlotte Gainsbourg and William Hurt

1997: directed by Robert Young, starring Samantha Morton and Ciaran Hinds

2006: directed by Susanna White, starring Ruth Wilson and Toby Stephens (BBC)

# Websites

www.haworth-village.org.uk/brontes/bronte.asp has pictures of Wycoller Hall, the model for Ferndean, the parsonage, showing the proximity of the graveyard, inside the parsonage, the walk to the Brontë waterfall, and more.

www.brontefamily.org is a webpage by Meredith Birmingham, containing a useful picture gallery.

www.wikipedia.org/wiki/Jane_Eyre has a basic introduction with plot summary, character list, themes and context.

www.victorianweb.org/authors/bronte/cbronte/jane1.html gives links to a variety of useful and interesting academic essays.

www.bronte.org.uk is the website of the Brontë Parsonage Museum and Brontë Society.

www.bbc.co.uk/drama/janeeyre is the BBC website about the making of its most recent dramatisation. It also gives a link to a website about the BBC production of *Wide Sargasso Sea* and to a *Woman's Hour* discussion about Jean Rhys.

www.bbc.co.uk/bradford/content/image_galleries/bronte_birthplace_thornton_gallery. shtml gives pictures of the birthplace of the Brontës in Thornton and links to other interesting sites.

www.sparknotes.com/lit/janeeyre is a useful introductory guide to the book with commentaries on each chapter.

assets.cambridge.org/97805217/70279/sample/9780521770279ws.pdf has an excellent essay by Juliet Barker on the Brontë family.